Now More Than Ever

"Social Studies" in the Twenty-first Century

James A. Bryant, Jr.

University Press of America,® Inc.
Lanham · Boulder · New York · Toronto · Plymouth, UK

Copyright © 2007 by
University Press of America,® Inc.
4501 Forbes Boulevard
Suite 200
Lanham, Maryland 20706
UPA Acquisitions Department (301) 459-3366

Estover Road
Plymouth PL6 7PY
United Kingdom

All rights reserved
Printed in the United States of America
British Library Cataloging in Publication Information Available

Library of Congress Control Number: 2006930311
ISBN-13: 978-0-7618-3553-0 (paperback : alk. paper)
ISBN-10: 0-7618-3553-9 (paperback : alk. paper)

∞™ The paper used in this publication meets the minimum
requirements of American National Standard for Information
Sciences—Permanence of Paper for Printed Library Materials,
ANSI Z39.48—1984

This book is dedicated to my grandmother, Garnell Bryant, whose love of history and gift for storytelling continue to inspire me, and to my wife, Ginger, who makes every word possible.

Table of Contents

Preface	vii
Acknowledgements	ix
Author's Note	xi
Chapter One Lorenzo's Revenge	1
Chapter Two "This will be all over Washington in 24 hours"	13
Chapter Three The Shadow of Colonel Tibbets	31
Chapter Four Avoiding the Bishop Trap	51
Chapter Five Beyond the Box	67
Chapter Six It's the Telephone Poles, Stupid	83
Select Bibliography	89
About the Author	92
Also by the Author	93

Preface

I suppose if I had any sense at all I would have entered law school. I would almost certainly make more money than I do in education and as the author of rare books. I would still read history books and watch documentaries, but I would not have taken on the responsibility and frustration of preparing future social studies teachers. But I did not choose that path or, more appropriately, that path did not choose me.

The frustration of which I speak has almost nothing to do with the young men and women I teach. Whether in Grand Forks, ND, New Orleans, LA, or now Boone, NC, the students are always the reason I get out of bed in the morning and enjoy coming in to work. Maybe I have been luckier than most—I can't say—but my students are the best and brightest, and they are committed to preserving and passing on the great stories of mankind to the next generations. They are most assuredly not the problem. They are heading into a system, however, that values compliance over conscience and that seems determined to break the spirit of young and idealistic teachers. If the dreadful statistics about the career longevity (or lack thereof) of new teachers is any indication, the system is winning. Young teachers enter into the classroom fired with a sense of idealistic daring, but these flames are all-too-quickly doused with the cold water of standards, paper work, end-of-grade standardized tests, federal, state and local politics, and a myriad of other things that have much to do with *Education* and nothing at all to do with teaching.

In this sorry state, we have reduced the power of the past to a mass of trivial nuggets that some narrow bureaucrat has determined one must know in order to be classified as "educated" by the state. Perhaps this is the unavoidable byproduct of placing the transmission of America's revolutionary pedigree into the hands of the State, which is—here as everywhere—concerned primarily with maintaining its power. Thus Jefferson, who believed and wrote that each generation should make their own laws rather than be governed by those of their parents' generation, is neutered and transformed into a shuffling old patriot who smiles benignly down upon us from our own Mount Olympus. He hurls no thunderbolts from this perch, and his world-altering polemics are watered down to the point of becoming, God help us, quaint. We test to make certain that students know that the Declaration of Independence was signed on July 4, 1776 (not entirely true of itself, but we'll leave that be for now), but we make no connection to this fact and their daily lives and struggles. Do we tell them that the young men and women who were murdered in Tiananmen Square in Beijing, China, were cut down by those bullets while clutching copies of our Declaration? The question then becomes: If not, why not? Isn't such a story the proof that our curriculum still has relevance?

And so we come to *Now More Than Ever*. It is my hope that this book will be in some way a contribution to the reformation of the way in which we teach history in this country. You will not find much on lesson plans and centering your world around your particular state's standard course of study, or whatever it is called wherever you are teaching. Lesson planning has to be the single most overblown "skill" that is "taught" in schools of education across the country. It doesn't take a scholar to figure it out, so I will leave you on your own for that. What you will find is my own belief that there is much work that needs to be done in order for the teaching of history to become what it needs to be, as well as my philosophy and prescription for making those changes. I do not pretend to believe that my ideas will cure all that ails our profession, but I do hope that they may serve as a conversation starter for reformers everywhere.

From this tentative beginning, I hope we can begin—all of us involved in teaching history at all levels of the educational system—to reclaim the story of America from the ideologues and idiots. That may be a daunting task, to be sure, but it is one we have to face. Each and every American has a stake in the portrayal of his or her nation, for it ultimately is the story of who we are and hope to be. History is a narrative that is too important to be left to the elites or to unqualified pedants. It is also a narrative that we all need to hear, to remind us of our values, our freedoms, our rights and responsibilities. Now, indeed, more than ever.

James A. Bryant, Jr.
February 2006
Todd, North Carolina

Acknowledgements

In any effort like this—whether a small book, big book, article or pamphlet—there are always numbers of people whose support made it possible. I would like to thank them all, and hope that I will not overlook any one. First, I would like to thank my friends and colleagues at the University of New Orleans, who continue to persevere amid challenges and obstacles that are incredibly daunting. Among all these folks I must single out Renee Casbergue, Pat Austin, Andy Talmadge and John Daniel. I am extraordinarily grateful to Roger DeSanti, a terrific mentor and friend.

Many thanks also to Kevin Bryant, whose conversations keep me honest and vigilant against intellectual apathy or certitude.

In order to write anything, you need a quite place to lay out all your books and notes and to slave over the keyboard without (too much) distraction. I am very appreciative of the efforts of the "Rayfield Boys," Harold, Rodney, and Colt, for literally building me my writing space.

My new friends and colleagues at Appalachian State University have been great support as I prepared this manuscript, and I am appreciative of their help and assistance.

The person to whom I am most indebted, as usual, is my wife Ginger. Thank you for reading each and every version of each and every chapter of this manuscript, making thoughtful suggestions, and generally making it a better work. To my children—Cheyenne, Autumn and James—thank you for understanding the hours Dad spent in the basement or the library.

Finally, I would like to say "thank you" to Jim Kennedy. Mr. Kennedy was my teacher in high school, and he is the reason I became a teacher myself. Those words—*thank you*—seem so small in light of the spiritual, intellectual, and emotional debt I owe you. I carry you with me every time I step into my own classroom, and I give it my all while trying to carry on your work. Thank you for inspiring a boy from Locust to drink deeply from life and to dare to glance across the county line.

Acknowledgements

Quotations from Alfred North Whitehead reprinted with permission of Scribner, an imprint of Simon and Schuster Adult Publishing Group from *The Aims of Education and Other Essays* by Alfred North Whitehead. Copyright ©1929 by The Macmillan Company; copyright renewed ©1957 by Evelyn Whitehead.

Author's Note

Throughout this book, the words "history" and "social studies" are used interchangeably. My philosophy, as will become clear throughout the text, is that the curricular focus on the historical discipline, while supported and enriched by the other social sciences, is the proper focus of what we call *social studies*. That is the reason for the word usage.

We dare not forget today that we are the heirs of that first revolution.

~ President John F. Kennedy

Chapter One
Lorenzo's Revenge

I have two strong spiritual ties to what is now Hampton University in Virginia. One is familial, the other professional. My great-great grandfather, Lorenzo Dow Swayney, was taken from his home on the Cherokee Indian reservation in western North Carolina to be educated and "civilized" at the Hampton Institute in the 1890s (which became present-day Hampton University). I keep a picture of him in my office at Appalachian State University that was taken during his time there. It is the same photograph that graces the front cover of this book. His hair has been cut and he has been placed in a suit for the photograph. His eyes have a far-away, lonely look about them. This is not surprising, since administrators at Hampton "believed the dominant failing of Indians to be an excessive and largely unwarranted amount of racial pride."[1] Samuel Chapman Armstrong, founder of the Hampton Institute, once bragged that he had "lassoed wild Indians all to be cleaned and tamed by a simple process I have invented known as the 'Hampton method.'"[2] This method was determined to rid American Indian students of that "excessive" pride in their people and themselves. My great-great grandfather's lonely eyes seem to speak volumes about the consequences of this effort.

My professional tie to the Hampton Institute comes from the fact that I am a professor of "social studies education," which means that I am in the business of training future social studies teachers. In 1902 a Welshman named Thomas Jesse Jones came to Hampton as an associate chaplain and head of the Economics and Missionary department.[3] Jones would become the founder of American "social studies." He "was probably the first person to teach a course called 'the social studies'...Jones believed that history was useless to poor minorities; it was not history study that they needed, but the right sort of skills and attitudes to fit them into the existing social order."[4]

Jones no doubt brought some of this philosophy with him from Great Britain. The term social studies appears to have originated there. In the 1830s a social welfare movement in England arose from the societal problems arising from that nation's shift from an agrarian to an industrial society. These problems grew as the urban population expanded.[5] Jones "had been exposed to country living, rural trades, and the problems of community adjustment even before his 1884 immigration" to the United States.[6] His theories would find fertile ground in America, where many educators sought a way to successfully acculturate the waves of immigrants that began arriving in the middle and latter period of the nineteenth century.

In fact, long before Jones rose to prominence, William McGuffey's readers were being used to show students (and, to some extent, parents) the proper behavior and thoughts of cultured Americans.[7] Conway MacMillan of the University of Minnesota argued for "social education," a course of study he believed could allow the schools to meet their responsibility for promoting students as social beings. MacMillan characterized the goal of social education as making young Americans "sensitive to the needs of the group as opposed to the promotion of self-interest."[8]

As defined by these early proponents, social studies addressed "society's need to pass on the cultural heritage (major ideas and values of a people) from one generation to the next."[9] The school was the one institution common to all Americans. Unlike religious or political institutions all students, it was assumed, would have equal or, at least, comparable experiences in their schooling. For this reason it seemed obvious that the place to inculcate traditional values such as patriotism was the school house. Even liberal educators like John Dewey discussed the need to form curricula "in which a social group brings up its immature members into its own social forms."[10] What was needed was a subject area that would accomplish this feat.

Thus began the battle between those who wanted the study of history (they called it "social education") to be used for the indoctrination of America's young, and those who wanted a rigorous and accurate study of history in the schools. Those arguing for an objective academic study of history in elementary and secondary schools were set up for defeat in 1893, when the National Education Committee of Ten (also known as the Madison Conference) attempted to define a set curriculum for the study of history. The academics at this conference ignored the popular sentiment that history should be jingoistic and rather emphasized that history "should emphasize 'scientific' history over 'patriotic' history."[11] The committee argued that such study would better prepare students for college admissions than a flag waving look at the past. The American Historical Association's (AHA) Committee of Seven seconded this curriculum in 1899. In 1905, the AHA's Committee of Eight recommended that the study of "Old World" history (Europe) be added to the sixth grade curriculum as a prelude to the study of American history.[12] But there was a backlash against this view of history; many believed it did not present the American story in a properly positive tone. The stage was set for Thomas Jesse Jones.

Upon arriving at Hampton, Jones ran a campaign against educators such as W.E.B. DuBois who argued that minorities needed an academic foundation as much as vocational training. DuBois mocked the philosophy of those such as Jones who wanted to limit the education of minorities to practical matters. He summed up his view of Jones' philosophy with this withering piece of satire: "Take the eyes of these millions off the stars and fasten them in the soil; and if their young men will dream dreams, let them be dreams of corn bread and molasses."[13]

Jones saw the study of history as a dangerous course of action where minorities were concerned. After all, what might happen if the African-Americans and American Indians under his tutelage began to take seriously propositions such as "All men are created equal?" In accordance with his beliefs, Jones formed a course of study he called "social studies" that would discourage students from questioning the social order. Rather, he saw his courses as a way to prepare students for taking their place within the status quo. These courses were indeed revolutionary, since the "Hampton course of studies...may have been the first anywhere to unite such diverse disciplines as civics, political economy, history, and sociology, and certainly was the first to apply them to race."[14] Lindsey writes that "the historical part of Jones's civics course proffered Armstrong's position that enslaving blacks and dispossessing Indians had been justifiable: conquest, history showed, was 'natural' because it had civilized new peoples."[15]

Jones couched his theories on history in terms progressive educators of the time could appreciate. He argued that the study of history needed to be replaced with something that had as its ultimate goal the creation of "good citizens." Jones "thought that education should adjust youngsters to their society and their prospects."[16] Too much of history dealt with men and women bending and changing their society when it failed them—a dangerous ideal to place in a student's head. For Jones, social studies was the answer, and he viewed this new subject as one that would "teach youngsters the right attitudes and adjust them to the industrial order."[17] As Ravitch summed it up, for Jones "history was far too individualistic, and its results not predictable."[18]

In 1916, Jones' theories about social studies expanded beyond their Hampton borders and became the national norm. In this year Jones led a National Education Association committee that had been brought together to face the challenge of making secondary schooling more relevant and effective. This was a landmark conference for social studies education, because it found (no doubt thanks to Jones' influence) that the study of history was no longer enough to prepare students for enlightened citizenship. Thus, "social studies" replaced history in the curriculum. In the ensuing years, students have been faced with a strange and meandering potpourri of activities and curricula that best resembles what educator Alan Nevins once referred to as "social slush."[19]

ଔ

The "Hampton Method" was an abject failure where my great-great grandfather was concerned. Lorenzo Dow Swayney appears to have had enough of that pride Samuel Chapman railed against to have made him all but impervious to efforts at breaking his Cherokee spirit. He returned to the reservation and became a confidante of chiefs and a power broker among his people. He not only continued to speak his native tongue, but he insisted on teaching that language to his children and grandchildren. He compromised only a little—reading the Christmas story from the New Testament each Christmas Eve in both

Cherokee *and* English. One imagines this is hardly the outcome Armstrong and Jones had envisioned.

Thomas Jesse Jones' efforts at giving "social studies" more prominence than history was more successful. But his twin goals, that of creating malleable products who would unquestioningly take their place within society as it was already constructed, and also developing good citizens were, in fact, mutually exclusive. Sadly, and to the detriment of the nation, it was the malleable product which emerged from the new social studies curriculum and not the enlightened or involved citizen. And why not? As taught, history is a record of successes virtually without effort—the outcome is never really in doubt. America always stands on the side of good, and her enemies, whether Plains Indians or Eastern European communists, are always on the side of evil. America always manages to get the leaders we need in time of crisis, and democracy always prevails.

There is very little in the current teaching of social studies to make any young person feel that it might be incumbent upon him or her to hone thinking skills or to even become involved in matters of state. If we simply take our place in line without raising a ruckus or questioning too many things, Lynne Cheney will tell us again and again how lucky we are to be Americans, and someone in the government will tell us what being an American means. *Social Studies*, that strange amalgam of history and every other social science imaginable, has become pure tedium for our students. The result is that they see no value in their nation's history, and no reason to raise their voices in making a little history of their own. Barr, Barth and Shermis have rightly called social studies a "schizophrenic bastard child."[20] The tragic result of Jones' success is that America has allowed several generations to develop a benign contempt for history.

This result is obvious to any social studies teacher who is willing to notice. The students arrive to our classes in the latest fashions and with a look on their face that clearly states their opinion that our class will be the most boring and least useful hour of their day. They are here not by choice, but to fulfill the minimal requirements set by their state for graduation. Once these are met, most of these students will never again take even a passing interest in history. They will scarcely ever open the pages of a biography, unless it is one of the myriad of works that gets published each year detailing the sexual exploits of John F. Kennedy, cataloging the numerous anxiety disorders of the beautiful but deeply-flawed Princess of Wales, or the obligatory tome on the secret alliance between former President Clinton and the devil. Some of these works may make it into the satchel they carry to the beach, but most likely even these books will come in a distant second to the latest thriller by John Grisham or the tantalizing tales of Danielle Steele.

And yet the nation survives, begging the question, "Does history really matter?" After all, standardized tests show year after year that history is the subject on which students score the lowest, but America continues to be the lone "superpower" in the world. Is this evidence that those of us decrying the lack of historical knowledge among our fellow citizens are just academic Chicken Littles? Could Thomas Jesse Jones have been correct in his assessment that we need only educate our young enough to provide them with marketable skills and attitudes? The answer, I believe, is an absolute and unqualified "no." History matters. History, like time, waits for no man, and stops for no man. The only question is whether or not we shall be participants or victims. But rhetoric alone does not make a case. So let us look at some examples from our recent past that may shed some light on why history matters, and the danger that is inherent in the development of a passive populace, such as has been the effect of modern "social studies" learning.

The Death of a President

On November 22, 1963, President John Fitzgerald Kennedy was murdered in Dallas, Texas. That much Americans know. Beyond that simple and tragic fact, however, lays a web of mystery and intrigue worthy of any Shakespearean drama. On November 29, 1963, one week after the murder, Kennedy's successor, Lyndon Baines Johnson, set up a commission to establish the facts surrounding the assassination.[21] The Warren Commission, as it has come to be known, had one true item on its agenda: put this case to bed quickly. Truth was not as high on the list of priorities as was an efficient vindication of federal agencies and the need for something that would ease the mind of the public that Lee Harvey Oswald was the only assassin. J. Edgar Hoover, the director of the Federal Bureau of Investigation at the time of Kennedy's killing, told one of Johnson's aides, "The thing I am most concerned about...is having something issued so we can convince the public that Oswald is the real assassin."[22] It would seem the commission's outcome was preordained.

Despite the incredible arrogance and near-comic presumption of author Gerald Posner, the assassination of John F. Kennedy is not "case closed." There remain a plethora of valid questions being asked by serious scholars. Was the president of the United States the victim of a one-in-a-million shot fired by a "lone nut" assassin, or was Kennedy the victim of a more insidious conspiracy? Kennedy's brother, Attorney General Robert F. Kennedy, had as his first response to learning of the president's murder a belief that the CIA may have been involved.[23] Over the years, other theories (some credible, many outlandish) have involved organized crime, Castro, Lyndon Johnson, and sundry combinations of all.

To be fair, I grow more and more suspicious of the conspiracy theories the older I get. In light of the wild stories surrounding the untimely death of Princess Diana, I have become more convinced that we have a need to protect ourselves from the random nature of much of history, and one of the ways we do this is by developing webs of drama and intrigue to combat the often banal, though tragic, twists of historic fate. Still, I do not know who killed President Kennedy or who was behind it. That is the crux of the matter. The government's rush to judgment and a paternalistic need to "protect" the American people is as responsible as any bit of human nature for the theories that continue to surround the death of Kennedy. Year after year polls indicate that large majorities of the American public do not believe the findings of the Warren Commission. The people know that their duly-elected leader was killed, feel that the government somehow covered up the facts surrounding the case, and yet we go about our business as if nothing untoward had happened. In a democracy, such apathy may well be the beginning of the end.

Starr Wars

In 1992 Arkansas governor William Jefferson Clinton defeated the incumbent, George Herbert Walker Bush, for the presidency of the United States. From the moment Clinton took office, powerful right-wing forces sought to destroy him and his presidency. The effort began as an investigation into a real estate deal Clinton and his wife had been part of while he was governor of Arkansas. The Whitewater land deal would turn into one of the longest running and most disgraceful political witch hunts in modern American history.

In the end, no evidence of malfeasance was found against President or Mrs. Clinton with regard to the failed real estate venture. But an over-zealous and highly partisan special prosecutor named Kenneth Starr managed to morph the investigation in such ways that the American people eventually spent over forty million dollars to discover that, while this president indeed was not a crook, he was a lousy husband.

On January 12, 1994, Clinton announced that he wanted a special counsel to be named to fully investigate his Whitewater land dealings so that the matter could be put to rest as quickly as possible. His attorney general, Janet Reno of Florida, chose sixty-three year old Robert Fiske.[24] Fiske laid out his plans simply and concisely for the investigative team working for him:

> He [Fiske] was not going to bring marginal cases, he was not going to see his investigation politicized, and most of all he was not going to take seven years. They were going to work fourteen hours a day seven days a week, determine if there were any crimes to prosecute, bring their cases, and then go home.[25]

This would seem like an imminently reasonable method of investigation. But it was not enough to satisfy the right-wing effort to unseat Clinton.

The independent counsel law invoked by Clinton and put into motion by Reno had a loophole that would allow the president's enemies to put a more dogmatic investigator on the case. The loophole provided that the choice of independent counsel be approved by a "Special Division." This Special Division was a committee of judges who had no real guidelines upon which to judge the selection of the attorney general. Thus, it was something of a surprise when, on August 5, 1994, the Special Division fired Fiske and hired Kenneth W. Starr.[26]

Judge David Sentelle was one of the judges on the Special Division. *The Washington Post* reported that Sentelle had lunched on July 14 with North Carolina senators and über-conservatives Jesse Helms and Lauch Faircloth, both rabid and avowed enemies of the new president. Although all parties denied that there had been any discussion of the Fiske matter, as Toobin states, "The timing of the lunch suggested that the senators were lobbying Sentelle to dump Fiske—which the judge promptly did."[27] Toobin goes to write that:

> In fact, behind the scenes, the three-judge panel was engaged in a decorous struggle over the Whitewater independent counsel—one that, again, revealed the political roots of this fight. Sentelle and Judge Joseph Sneed, who were both Republicans, wanted Fiske replaced with Starr. They thought the appointment by Reno had fatally compromised Fiske, giving his continued supervision of the case the 'appearance of impropriety,' but they saw no such problems with appointing an outspoken Republican opponent of Clinton's like Starr.[28]

Toobin describes Starr as "a committed political conservative who stood outspokenly opposed to Clinton on virtually every controversial issue of the day."[29] Starr's right-wing ties included *The American Spectator*, the Bradley Foundation and the Washington Legal Foundation.[30] Starr had also represented both *Brown and Williamson* and *Philip Morris*, two tobacco firms "whose interests clashed with the Clinton administration's at every step."[31] So much for the *independent* counsel.

For all his messianic fervor, the best Starr could do was discover that Clinton had engaged in oral sex with a White House intern named Monica Lewinsky. Exactly what bearing this revelation had on the Whitewater land deal, Starr never bothered to answer. His report, one of the more salacious pieces of government writing of all time, led to impeachment proceedings against Clinton which were easily beaten back. On February 12, 1999, the United States Senate declined the opportunity presented to them by Starr—to overturn two national elections and remove Bill Clinton from office. Describing Starr's methods, Toobin writes of the "vengefulness of Starr's prosecutors" and their "unhealthy obsession with getting the president."[32]

Despite the national disgrace that was the Whitewater witch-hunt, the American people seemed to take the whole sorry mess in stride. There seemed to be a pathetic sense that this was politics—this was the best we could or should expect from our leaders. They were petty, weak and silly, but who were we to demand more? A nation better schooled in their own powerful history might have been better able to answer that question.

Padlocking the Memory Hole

Prior to the administration of Richard M. Nixon, there had been no real thought as to whether or not the official papers of a president belonged to the chief executive or the American people. Because Nixon's documents were also potential evidence in criminal cases, Congress and the judicial branch found themselves trying to lay claim to what had, from the time of Washington, been the personal property of the man leaving office. The result of this bureaucratic mess was the Presidential Records Act of 1978. This act made the papers of a presidential administration the ultimate property of the American people and held that they "should be made publicly available within a sensible period of time."[33] Congress allowed former presidents up to twelve years to use their papers for memoirs, and then the material was to be opened to the public.

The first president to whom this law applied was Ronald Reagan (and, by extension, his vice president, George H.W. Bush). Most of the 40 million pages held by the Reagan Library have already been opened to researchers and historians. However, the library sought to keep 68,000 pages locked away for the entire twelve year period.[34] On January 21, 2001, all records dealing with the Reagan administration should have, by law, been open to historical scrutiny.

But a strange thing happened on the way to the archives. In January 2001, George W. Bush, son of Reagan's vice president, became president. The new president's White House lawyers asked for "an extension so they could review the 'many constitutional and legal questions' relating to these documents. Then they asked for another, and then another."[35] What exactly these "constitutional and legal questions" were, no one seems to know. As famed Watergate figure John Dean writes, "One can only presume Bush's wariness may have something to do with what those papers say about his father or members of his administration."[36]

Not content with delaying the release of these presidential papers through constant stonewalling, George W. Bush issued Executive Order No. 13223 on November 1, 2001. This order "created an entirely new set of procedures for handling presidential papers and imposed new access standards never fathomed by Congress."[37] Essentially, President Bush "was repealing an act of Congress and imposing a new law by executive fiat."[38] Lawsuits have been filed by the American Civil Liberties Union and the American Historical Association, but at the time of this writing the papers remain sealed in a sort of legal limbo.

The consequences are obvious. By ignoring the will (and authority) of Congress, Bush has made the work of historians and those who advocate an open government immensely more difficult. The veil of secrecy that he and his administration have pulled down around the executive branch is perilous for democracy, and yet most Americans are completely unaware that this fight is even being waged. It is our government, of course, but one would not think so from the efforts of the Bush team and their lawyers. Without the outcry of the people, Executive Order No. 13223 has become the law of the land. It sets sweeping new precedents that build a tremendous wall between the government and the governed. This order provides, among other things, that former presidents can keep their papers sealed indefinitely, and the burden of proof now falls on those wishing to view presidential records.[39] Orwell would be proud.

America's (Fill in the Blank) Media

It has long been an accepted truism that America's national media is controlled by a liberal elite. Former Presidents Richard Nixon and Ronald Reagan both made significant political hay by playing up (some might say inventing) this idea. In recent years the American political left has fought back, pointing to examples such as Fox News to show that the media is, in fact, conservative.

The facts would seem to show that our media is neither left nor right, but rather shallow and cynical. In the 2000 campaign, for instance, research done by the Pew Charitable Trusts Project for Excellence in Journalism shows that Republican George W. Bush "was twice as likely as [Democrat Al] Gore to get coverage that was positive in tone."[40] It seems quite odd that a "liberal" media would lavish such kind and positive coverage on the Republican nominee. The chart below shows a breakdown of the tone of the coverage during the final, key weeks of the campaign.

Tone of Coverage for Gore & Bush

	Gore	Bush
Positive	13%	24%
Neutral	31	27
Negative	56	49
Total	100%	100%

As can be seen from the chart, Bush's coverage, while more positive than Gore's, was still far from rosy. Bush's negative coverage was twice that of his positive, and Gore's negative coverage was an astonishing *five times* that of his positive.[41] Clearly then, the American media is conservative in its slant, right? Not really.

The 2004 presidential campaign shows almost the exact opposite of what was seen in 2000. In 2004, Democratic challenger John F. Kerry was more likely to receive positive coverage than the incumbent. The Project for Excellence in Journalism found that "More than half of all Bush stories studied were decidedly negative in tone. By contrast, only a quarter of all Kerry stories were clearly negative."[42] Positive coverage of Kerry accounted for 34% of his press, while only 14% of Bush's coverage was positive (as compared to a whopping 59% negative). So what gives? Did the liberal media just dislike Gore?

The answer is more complex and more depressing. The study of the coverage of the 2000 and 2004 elections found that the media was far less likely to focus on issues of policy or philosophical differences between the candidates, and more likely to focus on "internal campaign matters like tactics, strategy, candidate performance and horse race" issues.[43] The media has managed to reduce matters of civic importance to mere gamesmanship. The medium has indeed become the message. The study found that in 2004, "Despite what many consider striking contrasts offered by the two candidates, just over one in ten stories (13%) were framed around explaining issues."[44] A presidential campaign where only 13% of the press coverage is actually about policy differences! Little wonder, then, that the American people rarely see a difference between the two major party nominees. This number was down from an already anemic 27% in the 2000 election.[45] The media focuses not on ideas, ideals, or principles, but on tactics. This reflects neither a conservative nor a liberal bias, but rather sloppy sensationalism.

While labels such as "liberal" and "conservative" do not accurately describe the national media, there is one label that would seem to fit: oligarchy. The American ideal of freedom of the press is now concentrated in fewer and fewer corporate hands. One example should suffice. Eric Alterman points out that:

> When AOL took over TimeWarner, it also took over: Warner Brothers Pictures, Morgan Creek, New Regency, Warner Brothers Animation, a partial stake in Savoy Pictures, Little Brown & Co., Bullfinch, Back Bay, Time-Life Books, Oxmoor House, Sunset Books, Warner Books, the Book-of-the-Month Club, Warner/Chappell Music, Atlantic Records, Warner Audio Books, Elektra, Warner Sub-Pop records, *Time* magazine, *Fortune, Life, Sports Illustrated, Vibe, People, Entertainment Weekly, Money, In Style, Martha Stewart Living, Sunset, Asia Week, Parenting,* Weight Watchers, *Cooking Light,* DC Comics, 49 percent of Six Flags theme parks, Movie World and Warner Brothers parks, HBO, Cinemax, Warner Brothers Television, partial ownership of Comedy Central, E!, Black Entertainment Television, Court TV, the Sega channel, the Home Shopping Network, Turner Broadcasting...New Line Cinema, Fine Line Cinema...Castle Rock Productions, CNN, CNN Headline News, CNN International, CNN/SI, CNN Airport Network, CNNfi, CNN radio, TNT, WTBS and the Cartoon Network.[46]

This is but one example; it says nothing about other media hegemonies such as Viacom, Sinclair Broadcasting, Disney and Westinghouse. What the American people will learn about their government is controlled by vast corporate entities, and that surely is not what the Founders had in mind when toiling over the Bill of Rights. As Bob Dole once asked, "Where is the outrage?"

Thomas Jesse Jones has been a remarkable success. Young Americans are not trained to question, and therefore they take their place as passive and docile adults. This is not citizenship. The course of study that should prepare young people for the challenges of citizenship in a democratic society—"social studies"—is a curricular mess, with no clear direction and no narrative that would allow students to prepare for making their voice heard in the marketplace of ideas. It is time for revolutionary change. America needs dedicated, thoughtful, active citizens now more than ever, and the drastic reformation of our "social studies" curriculum is the most logical place to begin. Young Americans must know the price that has been paid for the freedoms they enjoy. They must know how precious—and fragile—are these freedoms. The price of democracy is constant vigilance, and we must train students for this responsibility.

This book will examine three critical ways to reform the teaching of social studies in American schools. The first is to place the subject of history back in the place of primacy it deserves. Second, we must teach this history through a constructivist pedagogy that will allow students' much needed practice in refining and articulating their beliefs. Finally, the study of history must be done in a meaningful, multicultural way that prepares students for viewing America's role in a broader global context.

If we fail to reform social studies education, we risk continuing down a path of national apathy and malaise. The time is now, and the work to be done is daunting, but a glance at our history shows that we are up to the task.

Postman and Weingartner point out that "Santayana told us that a fanatic is someone who redoubles his efforts when he has forgotten his aim."[47] The aim of social studies must be to prepare America's young for leadership—not Jones' goal of preparing them for a lifetime of following.

My great-great Grandfather spent his years after the Hampton Institute overcoming—not benefiting by—his education. I fear such is the case for American social studies students today. We can do better; we *must* do better. Ignorance of our heritage is not acceptable in a democracy. As Thomas Jefferson told us, "History, by apprising [students] of the past will enable them to judge the future; it will avail them of the experience of other times and other nations; it will qualify them as judges of the actions and designs of men; it will enable them to know ambition under every disguise it may assume; and knowing it, to defeat its views...Every government degenerates when trusted to the rulers of the people alone."[48] With this in mind, let the process of reform begin.

---

1 Donal F. Lindsey, *Indians at Hampton Institute 1877-1923* (Chicago: University of Illinois Press, 1995), 111.
2 Ibid, 112.
3 Ibid, 185.
4 Diane Ravitch, "Who Prepares our History Teachers? Who Should Prepare our History Teachers?" Keynote Address, National Council for History Education, October 18, 1997.
5 Thomas L. Dynneson and Richard E. Gross, *Designing Effective Instruction for Secondary Social Studies* (Upper Saddle River, NJ: Merrill, 1999), 30.
6 Lindsey, 185.
7 Dynneson and Gross, 31.
8 Ibid, 11.
9 Margaret A. Laughlin and H. Michael Hartoonian, *Challenges of Social Studies Instruction in Middle and High Schools* (New York: Harcourt Brace College Publishers, 1995), 1.
10 John Dewey, *Democracy and Education: An Introduction to the Philosophy of Education* (New York: The Free Press, 1916), 10.
11 Dynneson and Gross, 26.
12 Ibid.

13 W.E.B. DuBois, *The Education of Black People: Ten Critiques, 1906-1960* (New York: Monthly Review Press, 1973), 9.
14 Lindsey, 186.
15 Ibid, 188.
16 Ravitch.
17 Ibid.
18 Ibid.
19 Dynneson and Gross, 39.
20 Robert Barr, James L. Barth and S. Samuel Shermis, *Defining the Social Studies*. Bulletin 51. (Washington, D.C.: National Council for the Social Studies, 1977), 1.
21 Arthur M. Schlesinger, Jr., *Robert Kennedy and his Times* (New York: Ballantine Books, 1978), 662.
22 Ibid, 663.
23 Ibid, p.665.
24 Jeffrey Toobin, *A Vast Conspiracy: The Real Story of the Sex Scandal That Nearly Brought Down a President* (New York: Random House, 1999), 71.
25 Ibid.
26 Ibid, 72.
27 Ibid, 73.
28 Ibid.
29 Ibid, 77.
30 Ibid.
31 Ibid.
32 Ibid, 396.
33 John W. Dean, *Worse Than Watergate: The Secret Presidency of George W. Bush* (New York: Little, Brown and Company, 2004), 89.
34 Ibid.
35 Ibid, 90.
36 Ibid.
37 Ibid.
38 Ibid.
39 Ibid, 91.
40 http://www.journalism.org/resources/research/reports/campaign2000/lastlap/default.asp
41 Ibid.
42 http://www.journalism.org/resources/research/reports/debateeffect/default.asp
43 Ibid.
44 http://www.journalism.org/resources/research/reports/debateeffect/winners%20and%20losers.asp
45 http://www.journalism.org/resources/research/reports/campaign2000/lastlap/default.asp
46 Eric Alterman, *What Liberal Media? The Truth About Bias and the News* (New York: Basic Books, 2003), 22-23.
47 Neil Postman and Charles Weingartner, *Teaching as a Subversive Activity: A no-holds-barred assault on outdated teaching methods—with dramatic and practical proposals on how education can be made relevant to today's world* (New York: Delacorte Press, 1969), 13.
48 Laughlin and Hartoonian, 6.

Chapter Two
"This will be all over Washington in 24 Hours"

The fax machine roared to life, giving hope to every historian and history teacher in America. For weeks the committee assigned to investigate the terrorist attacks of September 11, 2001 in New York and Washington, D.C. had been requesting that the National Security Advisor for the administration of President George W. Bush, Condoleezza Rice, testify under oath before the commission. The administration had steadfastly denied the request, claiming that such testimony would set a dangerous precedent and might impede future presidents from getting open and unvarnished advice from aides. The struggle had reached a tense impasse, and it appeared that Dr. Rice would never testify. Then the committee's historian, Philip Zelikow, came to the rescue.

Michael Isikoff of *Newsweek* describes the scene like this:

> The grainy photograph rolled off the fax machine at the White House counsel's office...along with a scribbled note that smacked of blackmail. If the White House didn't allow national-security advisor Condoleezza Rice to testify in public...it read, "This will be all over Washington in 24 hours."[1]

The fax referred to a photograph Zelikow had found. The historian from the University of Virginia had discovered a picture of Admiral William D. Leahy—who had been chief of staff to presidents Franklin D. Roosevelt and Harry S. Truman—testifying before Congress on November 22, 1945. Leahy was appearing before a commission investigating the attack on Pearl Harbor. Moreover, the photograph had run on the front page of *The New York Times*.[2] The administration's claims of precedent immediately collapsed, and Dr. Rice eventually testified. 9/11 Commission co-chair Thomas Keane remarked, "This is what happens when you hire historians."[3]

This anecdote should be a great boon to those who teach history. It shows that historical knowledge can be power. Perhaps more to the point, it shows that the tools used and the skills honed through historical scholarship have an important function and are useful. Being a historian involves much more than looking misty eyed at ancient parchment. Zelikow's work brought needed accountability to the nation's executive branch. Such skills are necessary for every American citizen. These skills are poorly taught in today's social studies classrooms, however. With this in mind, this chapter focuses on the first reform outlined in the previous chapter, that of placing historical study back at the center of the curriculum.

&

The 1916 *National Education Association Commission on the Reorganization of Secondary Education: Committee on the Social Studies* was a watershed event for the study of history in American schools. This committee made the leap from the traditional study of history in the schools to the more amorphous curriculum of social studies. Again, the major premise behind this change was that the nation had a need to "bring the history curriculum in line with the push for more socially efficient and socially responsible schools."[4] The 1916 committee was also important because of its makeup; it was filled not with subject area specialists (historians, political scientists, geographers, etc.), but with "public school and university educators."[5] As Dynneson and Gross point out, "[t]his was the first time a national curriculum committee had been organized that was not composed largely of historians and social scientists."[6] The result was that the study of history was scaled back in favor of a more integrated approach that emphasized the dogmas of Thomas Jesse Jones.

Jones' ideas about history were not accepted without a fight, however. As the study of history receded into the background and the American school curriculum become a wasteland of pabulum formulated to indoctrinate rather than educate young people, there were brave and principled educators who stood up against the tide. One of these was Harold Rugg of Columbia University. Rugg chaired the National Society for the Study of Education's Committee on Curriculum Making, a body destined to do battle with Jones' legacy.[7] Rugg's philosophical view of the role of education in a democratic society was diametrically opposed to the view Jones had espoused. Rugg argued for a curriculum that would prepare students to change their social climate. He believed that there needed to be a fundamental movement that would "reconstruct" the curriculum; Rugg hoped that such reconstruction of the school would inexorably lead to a reconstruction of American economic, political and social life. The culmination of Rugg's work was the *Twenty-Sixth Yearbook*, a study whose purpose was to make explicit the need for an education that prepared the young to face and conquer inequality in America.[8]

Rugg and educators like him believed that the purposes of education were not to pass on cherished ideals and values, but to question the very essence of American existence and then use these questions to bring about significant societal change. Rugg even developed a set of reconstructionist social studies textbooks. Despite his Herculean efforts, however, Rugg was fighting a losing battle. His textbooks "came under attack by conservative interests, and Rugg was labeled a 'socialist.'"[9] Rugg must have seen some gallows humor in the irony; Karl Marx himself had written, "Where is the party in opposition that has not been decried as communistic by its opponents in power?"[10]

Although Rugg's efforts may have been altruistic in nature, he and his committee did immeasurable harm to the cause of history education in America. As World War Two closed and the communist threat became paramount in the minds of many American citizens and politicians, the idea of using the school for social change proved to be anathema for most educators. Then, on October 4, 1957, the Soviet Union launched *Sputnik* into orbit. This event convinced Americans "that the Russians had made a coup in an area where many Americans presumed continuing superiority—the application of scientific research to technological production."[11]

The study of history was affected by this event in two major ways. First, America now realized that the Soviet Union was to be a serious competitor in all arenas on the world stage. *Sputnik* made the Soviets a technological competitor, and cries were quickly heard about the need for drastic expansion and improvements in the teaching of math and science in our schools. The corollary was that social studies would now be forced into a secondary position within the curriculum. More importantly perhaps, since capitalism and democracy were at stake in this contest, it was more important than ever that social studies be taught in a way that defended the American Way. Critical thinking and social reconstruction would have to wait.

The social studies curriculum as it currently exists makes little sense to students or teachers. The effort to broaden the scope of history into something that was a buffet of all the social sciences has been an abject failure, leaving students with no clear focus or rationale for why they are studying a given topic at any point in their educational career. What is needed is the clear statement from educators that we are seeking to improve our students' knowledge of history. This statement must then be followed by concerted action in the schools. History must again become paramount.

This process began in 1987 with the development of the *Bradley Commission on History in the Schools*. This commission was created "in response to widespread concern over the inadequacy, both in quantity and quality, of the history taught in American classrooms."[12] Importantly, this was "the first national group to devote its attention exclusively to history in the schools. Indeed, the case for the importance of history had not been cogently and powerfully made since the 1890s, when the distinguished Committee of Ten reported on the entire high school experience."[13] The commission wrote in its final report that "History belongs in the school programs of all students, regardless of their academic standing and preparation, of their curricular track, or of their plans for the future."[14]

The Bradley Commission was also important for the makeup of its members. In addition to the historians among its members, the committee included "classroom teachers as full voting and deliberative members of a national policy-making group."[15] These educators were invited to participate to "bridge the gap between the school and the university."[16] The hope was that the intellectual and purposeful divide that had arisen as a result of the 1893 committee would not be repeated and could, in fact, be closed.

The Bradley Commission found that the study of history had been forced aside "While other social science disciplines and many new fields, such as sex and health education, driver education, and computer education, had expanded their roles in the curriculum."[17] Some of their findings were startling. For example, in 1987 15% of American high school students did not take a *single course* in the discipline of American history, and "at least 60 percent did not study either World history or Western civilization."[18] The importance and relevance of historical study had clearly been lost. In 1916 John Dewey had written that:

> ...geography and history supply subject matter which gives background and outlook, intellectual perspective, to what might otherwise be narrow personal actions or mere forms of technical skill. With every increase of ability to place our own doings in their time and space connections, our doings gain in significant content.[19]

It was clear from the work of the Bradley Commission that such skills were not being derived from the current state of history education. The commission highlighted the importance of history in American society by pointing out that "Unlike many other peoples, Americans are not bound together by a common religion or a common ethnicity. Our binding heritage is a democratic vision of liberty, equality, and justice."[20] Knowledge and respect for this vision was getting shunted aside as history fell farther down the curricular priority list.

A significant part of the problem has been the haphazard melding of history with the social sciences to construct a "social studies" curriculum. History, when taught properly, is the wedding of the past's story with the social sciences. The effort to force what is, in fact, a naturally occurring relationship has led to a watered down phenomenon that has no true rhyme or reason. It has packed each school year with a load of information that cannot be adequately taught in the allotted time, and this has diluted the effectiveness of what could be an otherwise challenging and rewarding course of study. More to the point, the effort to mandate a broader and more integrated approach—at the expense of history—has wreaked havoc with the curriculum patterns in social studies. The chart below shows the curricular mess social studies teachers have inherited.

The chart refers to the scope of social studies instruction as it developed over a thirty-year period from 1960 to 1990. It seems abundantly clear that there has been no movement towards any logical sequencing of events and subjects in the scholastic study of secondary social studies. The same is true for both elementary and middle school level social studies. This lack of direction is almost certainly a direct result of the trimming of historical content. The move away from traditional historical study towards a porous idea of a catch-all social science has forced to students and teacher alike to contend with a curriculum that has no logical or discernible pattern.

Grade Level	1960*	1990*
6	Western Culture	World Culture
7	European History	World Geography/History
8	United States History	United States History
9	Civics	Civics/World History
10	World History	World History
11	United States History	United States History
12	American Problems	American Government/Economics

SOURCE: *Project SPAN, as reported in Social Education, May 1980, by Superka, Hawke, and Mossissett. Council of State Social Studies Specialists Survey, 1993. Des Moines: Iowa State Department of Education.[21]

A second problem with this arrangement is that it gives the opposite impression of that which it was intended to foster. Rather than showing with any clarity the interconnectedness of the social sciences and history, this grouping of subjects seems to further divide the disciplines into their own special categories. Note again the categorization of the seventh grade curriculum: "world geography/history." Does this not give the impression that these are disciplines that have been arbitrarily combined? Why not simplify this subject to "world history?" Would leaving out the term "geography" make the subject somehow irrelevant to the study of world history? Can students understand the folly of Napoleon or Hitler without a solid grounding in the geography and climate of Russia? Can anyone imagine studying the Treaty of Tordesillas without a conversation about geography?

Moving to the subject of American history, we see the problem is amplified. Laughlin and Hartoonian have pointed out that "[m]ost learners tend to be historical isolates—cut off from the idea of a historical continuum."[22] As Dewey states:

> The past just as the past is no longer our affair. If it were wholly gone and done with, there would be only one reasonable attitude toward it. Let the dead bury their dead. But knowledge of the past is the key to understanding the present.[23]

It is nearly impossible to imagine, however, students connecting the study of the past to the present when they cannot connect the material in sixth grade to that of the seventh! In eighth grade, students begin their look at United States history. Ninth grade is dedicated to "civics and world history," whatever that means. Tenth grade offers up more world history. Then, in eleventh grade, after a two year absence, students return to the history of America. Twelfth grade is set aside for government and economics, but by senior year most states no longer require history, so this last course would be an elective that may or may not be taken.

It would be useful to ask where the "continuum" in this program of study is. There is sufficient information now that this kind of fragmentation does not serve the students well. A Harvard study "noted that the organization of the curriculum into rigid autonomous units results in students being unable to transfer their learnings from subject to subject."[24] In the strange world of social studies, it is doubtful that students can transfer their knowledge from year-to-year, and because of the sequencing, this would mean an inability to transfer learning *within the same subject*. Surely this is an unacceptable state of affairs.

In addition to the problems with the curriculum of modern social studies, there is also significant concern over the basic qualifications of those employed to teach the subject in American schools. Two studies produced in 1986 highlighted these issues. Those reports, *A Nation Prepared: Teachers for the 21st Century* (prepared by the Carnegie Forum on Education and the Economy) and *Tomorrow's Teachers* (prepared by the Holmes Group) called for "sweeping changes in teacher education and stimulated extensive debate over the appropriate content of teacher education."[25] The debate, which continues to this day, is over whether teachers should major in their primary content area or in the more generalized field of education. A report done by the National Center for Education Statistics (NCES) called *America's Teachers: Profile of a Profession, 1993-94* found that 45% of pre-service teachers majored in education, 7% in special education, and 1% in other educational fields. The remaining 47% majored in their content field (such as American history).[26] Specifically, 69% of all public elementary school teachers majored in general education, while 20% of public secondary school teachers did so.[27] Although the Bradley Commission focused its work on curriculum reform, it had the following to say about the current qualifications (or lack thereof) of too many social studies teachers:

> Precisely because so many history teachers are inspiring and effective, the Bradley Commission recognized the importance of their careful education and selection. We deplored the common practice, unfortunately still quite common, of assigning unqualified teachers to teach social studies in our schools. State certification alone is not a guarantee of competence, if only because in some states it is still possible to be certified to teach social studies without ever taking a single college course in history.[28]

The education of the teacher and their eventual teaching assignments also proved to be problematic. The NCES report discovered that in 1993-94, 8% of schools with teaching vacancies filled these positions with "a less than fully qualified teacher."[29] In this instance, "qualified" means that the teacher held either an academic major or minor in their main assignment field. In fact, 28% of teachers in public schools were teaching subjects for which they were not qualified. A depressing 36% of teachers in private schools were not qualified to teach in their assigned subject area.

Figure 2.1
Percentage of public and private school academic teachers who neither majored nor minored in main assignment field as undergraduates, by teaching field: 1993-94

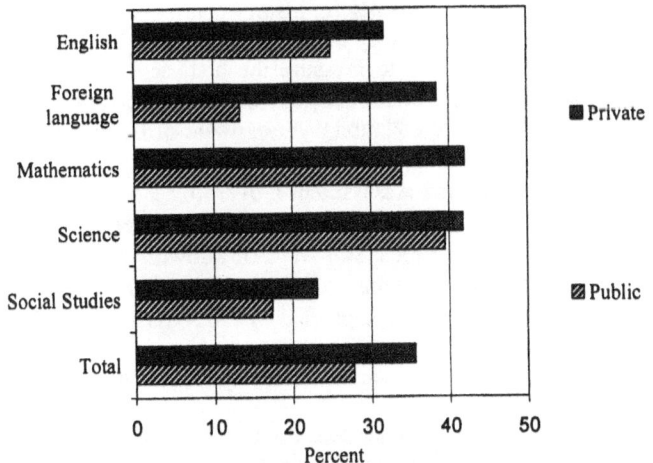

SOURCE: U.S. Department of Education. National Center for Education, Statistics, Schools and Staffing Survey: 1993-94 (Teacher Questionnaire)

For social studies, nearly one in five teachers in the public schools (17.4%) were not qualified to teach the area to which they had been assigned. In private schools, the number was nearly one-quarter (23.1%).[30]

These numbers continue to be a problem. In middle school (grades 5-8) in 1999-2000, "between 11 and 22 percent of the students enrolled in English, mathematics, science, foreign language, social science, and the subfield of history were in classes led by teachers without a major, minor, or certification in the subject taught."[31] In high school the number was between 5 and 7%. The chart below shows the number of teachers teaching outside of their field for history and social science.[32]

Subject Field	Middle Grades				High School Grades			
	No major and certification		No major, minor, or certification		No major and certification		No major, minor, or certification	
	1987-1988	1999-2000	1987-1988	1999-2000	1987-1988	1999-2000	1987-1988	1999-2000
Social Science	47.2	51.1	11.5	13.3	31.4	27.9	6.4	5.9
History	66.3	71.0	13.9	11.5	61.7	62.5	12.1	8.4

As the report states, about "one-half of the students in middle-grade social science classes (51 percent) had teachers who did not have a major and certification in the field, but 71 percent of the students in middle-grade history classes had teachers who did not report having a major in history or world civilization and certification in the field."[33] In high school, where the subjects are more specialized, an astounding 63% of students "in history classes did not have teachers with a major and certification in history or world civilization."[34]

Standardized test scores used to measure the historical understanding and proficiency of American youth reflect the poor quality of current social studies instruction. In 1994 and 2001 the National Assessment of Educational Progress tested students in fourth, eighth and twelfth grades to assess their knowledge of American history. The National Assessment Governing Board (NAGB) determined that "the assessment should be organized around three dimensions: historical themes, chronological periods, and ways of knowing and thinking about U.S. history."[35] The test was designed to measure these three results around four major themes. The themes, also identified by the NAGB, were:

1. Change and continuity in American democracy: ideas, institutions, practices and controversies;
2. The gathering and interactions of peoples, cultures, and ideas;
3. Economic and technological changes and their relation to society, ideas, and the environment; and
4. The changing role of America in the world.[36]

The test given to fourth, eighth and twelfth grade students finally sought to measure two specific "ways of knowing and thinking about U.S. history;" these were what the NAGB called "the cognitive dimension of the assessment."[37] The results of this standardized assessment, as Diane Ravitch noted, "were bleak."[38]

The test scores were divided into four categories: advanced, proficient, basic, and below basic. In both the 1994 and the 2001 results, a deplorable 57% of high school seniors taking the test scored below basic.[39] Of the remaining seniors, 43% scored at the level of basic, with another 11% scoring proficient. Only 1% of those taking the test received a score of advanced.[40]

The results for fourth and eighth grades were better, but still nothing to cause excitement among historians. In 1994, 36% of fourth graders scored below basic, with another 47% at the basic level of understanding. Only 17% scored at the proficient or advanced levels.[41] In 2001, these numbers had somewhat improved. These results showed that 49% of fourth graders now scored at the basic level, and the number scoring below basic had fallen to 33%. Still, one-third of fourth graders scoring so poorly in American history is hardly cause for celebration. Among eighth graders, the number of students scoring below basic dropped from 39% in 1994 to 36% in 2001. Those scoring at the advanced level moved from 1% to 2%, with 48% receiving a score of basic.[42] Of all the tests administered by the NAEP, the "results in history were worse than in any other subject area."[43]

For some perspective, it is useful to understand what the assessment considered advanced, proficient, basic and below basic. In fourth grade, 2% of students in 2001 scored at the advanced level. To reach this level a student needed to be able to, among other things, identify the branch of government responsible for passing laws, or explain the importance of one of the Founding Fathers.[44] Ninety-eight percent of American fourth graders found these questions too difficult.

Thus, it is clear that the current state of affairs in social studies is not getting the job done. American students have a very limited understanding of their heritage, and it is apparent that reform is needed immediately. The reforms called for by the Bradley Commission need to be implemented, and history needs to move to the very front of social studies education. In fact, it would be a valuable beginning to simply retire the term "social studies" for good. The Bradley Commission identified two main aims of American education: personal growth and active, intelligent citizenship. History speaks to both of these aims in powerful ways. As the commission noted, the study of history can play an important role in personal growth. History, after all, "is the central humanistic discipline. It can satisfy young people's longing for a sense of identity and of their time and place in the human story."[45]

As for the aim of intelligent and active citizenship, history "can convey a sense of civic responsibility by graphic portrayals of virtue, courage, and wisdom—and their opposites."[46] Hart has written that "America in the twenty-first century is a procedural republic deficient in the qualities of civic virtue, duty, citizen participation, popular sovereignty, and resistance to corruption."[47] Some may quibble with the severity of this indictment, but the sorry state of history education in America—as noted in the previously mentioned test scores—make one wonder how many young Americans would even understand what Hart is saying.

With these arguments as their foundation, the Bradley Commission set forth nine recommendations for the reform of social studies education. These recommendations were:

1. That the knowledge and habits of mind to be gained from the study of history are indispensable to the education of citizens in a democracy. The study of history should, therefore, be required of all students.
2. That such study must reach well beyond the acquisition of useful information. To develop judgment and perspective, historical study must often focus upon broad, significant themes and questions, rather than short-lived memorization of facts without context. In doing so, historical study should provide context for facts and training in critical judgment based upon evidence, including original sources, and should cultivate the perspective arising from a chronological view of the past down to the present day. Therefore it follows...
3. That the curricular time essential to develop the genuine understanding and engagement necessary to exercising judgment must be considerably greater than that presently common in American school programs in history.
4. That the kindergarten through sixth grade social studies curriculum be history-centered.

5. That this Commission recommends to the states and to local school districts the implementation of a social studies curriculum requiring no fewer than four years of history among the six years spanning grades 7 through 12.
6. That every student should have an understanding of the world that encompasses the historical experiences of peoples of Africa, the Americas, Asia, and Europe.
7. That history can best be understood when the roles of all constituent parts of society are included; therefore the history of women, racial and ethnic minorities, and men and women of all classes and conditions should be integrated into historical instruction.
8. That the completion of a substantial program in history (preferably a major, minimally a minor) at the college or university level be required for the certification of teachers of social studies in the middle and high schools.
9. That college and university departments of history review the structure and content of major programs for their suitability to the needs of prospective teachers, with special attention to the quality and liveliness of those survey courses whose counterparts are most often taught in the schools: world history, Western civilization, and American history.[48]

These suggestions are indeed sweeping and groundbreaking. They place history at the forefront of social studies education, and call on states and local government to make a genuine commitment to the teaching of the skills and dispositions provided by a solid history education.

The Bradley Commission was *not* suggesting, however, that we should toss aside the study of geography, economics, civics, or the other social sciences. These disciplines are, rather, part of the fundamental understandings that are the very foundation of history. One cannot, for example, accurately understand the American Revolution without a hefty dose of economics and geography. Indeed, the Commission's report stated that "Each kind of history provides a sturdy bridge to one or more of the social sciences and humanities."[49] While the subject currently called social studies needs to be reformed and the role of history greatly enhanced, the answer is not to ignore the other social sciences and their abilities to enrich and enhance the study of history in all its forms. The following curricular model may serve as a simple guide for what form this reform might take.

In this model, history is at the center of the curriculum. But the other social sciences (and this model is by no means all-inclusive) are brought to bear upon the study to bring richness and texture to history. The Bradley Commission wrote that history "is greatly enriched by concepts, insights, and illustrative materials from literature, biography and memoirs, psychology, economics, sociology, culture both high and popular, military and political science, film, drama, music and philosophy."[50] In the turf wars that are inevitable when curricular reform is attempted, we would do well to remember and emphasize this point.

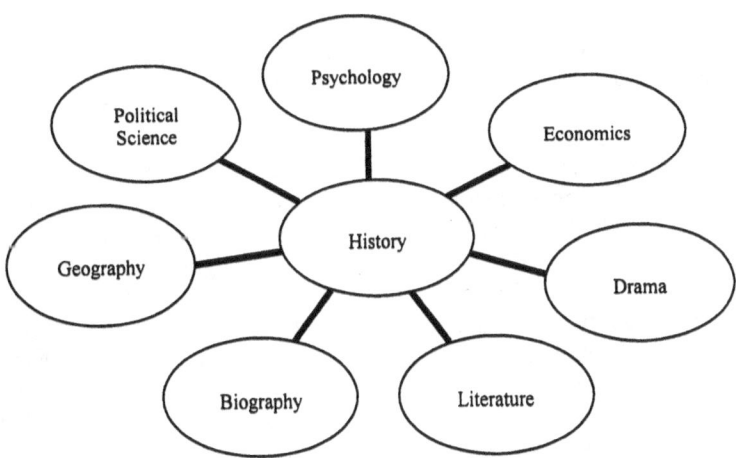

The beginning point of this curriculum reform must be the elementary school grades. At the moment, elementary school social studies is an embarrassment, focusing on a content-less curriculum of *expanding horizons*. The current approach "is not grounded in cognitive research on how children learn or in developmental studies of what they are capable of learning."[51] An example of this is the social studies textbook my daughter brought home in fourth grade. The textbook told students:

> Every one of you already holds the important office of citizen. Over time you will become more and more involved in your community. You will need to know more about what being a citizen means. Social studies will help you learn about citizenship.[52]

Perhaps this can happen, but not as a result of reading *this* textbook. The authors go on to define a citizen as someone who will "work to improve all the groups they belong to and to make the world a better place."[53] Yuck. Such saccharine is beneath the possibilities of fourth grade minds. No wonder my daughter complained that social studies bored her. While I do not contend that fourth graders can understand all the complexities of citizenship, I do emphatically contend that they are capable of more than the inane texts and activities that are the core of most elementary school social studies curricula.

There is nothing inherently wrong with the study of family, neighborhood and community in the early grades. But the way the curriculum is currently taught "is indifferent to historical instruction."[54] What a wasted opportunity! Young children love stories and adventures—and what is history if not the story and adventure of mankind? Here at these young ages educators have the opportunity to "hook" students onto the power and promise of history, and yet we do not. With a plethora of powerful children's books and young adult biographies, we have no excuse. In the interest of avoiding controversy and playing it safe, we sell short our youngest children, their abilities and their interests. Mary Beth Klee has said that "even our youngest students begin to be intuit and become excited about [history] when they embark, as I believe every child should, on the organized study of the human past."[55]

Elementary school-aged children are capable of more than coloring pictures of firemen and police, or making the obligatory grocery bag vest and construction paper headdress at Thanksgiving. "History," as the Bradley Commission reminds us, "offers a wide range of materials to delight and engage the young learner."[56] Allowing elementary students the chance to do serious work on local history, their family history and other such forms introduces the young learner to the scholarly foundations of historical study, and also may convince them of the usefulness of the subject—making the job of thousands of secondary teachers infinitely easier. Since history is no more or less than the story of mankind, the use of biography is another way to introduce the study of history to young children. The Bradley Commission said that "Teachers of young children should be encouraged to be storytellers and dramatists, not just monitors of basal readers or sociologists of the neighborhood."[57] If a goal of elementary social studies is to remain the expanding of horizons, then history is a powerful tool that has been ignored too long.

The Bradley Commission outlined three possible patterns of curriculum for the reform of elementary social studies education. These patterns emphasize history and provide a better sense of chronology than the modern curriculum. They are:

	Pattern A		Pattern B
Grade	Course	Grade	Course
K	Children of Other Lands and Times	K	Learning and Working Now and Long Ago
1	Families Now and Long Ago	1	A Child's Place in Time and Space
2	Local History: Neighborhoods and Communities	2	People Who Make a Difference
3	Urban History: How Cities Began and Grew	3	Continuity and Change: Local and National History
4	State History and Geography: Continuity and Change	4	A Changing State
5	National History and Geography: Exploration to 1865	5	United States History and Geography: Making a New Nation
6	World History and Geography: The Growth of Civilization	6	World History and Geography: Ancient Civilizations

Pattern C

Grade	Course
K	Children's Adventures: Long Ago and Far Away
1	People Who Made America
2	Traditions, Monuments, and Celebrations
3	Inventors, Innovators, and Immigrants
4	Heroes, Folk Tales, and Legends of the World
5	Biographies and Documents in World History
6	Biographies and Documents in World History

[58]

Although there are elements of each suggested pattern that could be improved upon, there is little doubt that these curricular patterns represent a tremendous improvement over the current elementary social studies curriculum. It is vital that the teaching of elementary social studies be improved because, as the old saying goes, you never get another chance to make a first impression. The first impressions current elementary school students get of social studies is of a hodge-podge curriculum that is boring and patronizing. This must change.

Middle and high school social studies is also in need of reform. The Bradley Commission wrote that:

> History should have special relevance for adolescents who are developing a sense of their own past as different from the present, struggling with problems of time's irreversibility in their own lives, searching for meaning and commitment for themselves, and redefining their relationship to society.[59]

Adolescence is a time of questioning, and the courses should make room for the development and articulation of opinions and beliefs. Secondary social studies should put the ghost of manifest destiny to rest for good, and allow students to see that history is not preordained, but that each success has been won through tremendous controversy and struggle. High school students need the study of history in order to understand their own responsibilities in a free society. The study of history provides more than a link to the past; it provides confirmation that humanity makes its own way through trial and error.

The Commission made a number of specific recommendations for the reform of secondary social studies. The most important of these in my estimation is for educators to "provide ways to relate each course to the other history courses that precede and follow it, throughout the curriculum."[60] This recommendation speaks directly to the isolation of information mentioned earlier in this chapter. They also called for an "ordered developmental sequence of increasing challenge and sophistication, based on current knowledge of learning styles and stages of intellectual development in students."[61] Thus, the new curriculum would be based on a foundation of chronological study; this is something which makes great sense when the topic is the study of history, and it is remarkable that such reform has not been implemented. The Commission offered the four curricular models below as possibilities.

It is of the utmost importance that secondary students receive a challenging and rich education in history. This is the last historical training many of them will ever get before taking their place as full member of our democracy. We do not have the luxury of sending these young men and women out full of ignorance of their heritage, their rights and their duties. For those preparing for a college education, we owe it to them to prepare them for the rigor and uncertainty of college history classes. We currently fail both sets of students.

It is perhaps the university partnerships that hold the most promise for improving the training of pre-service social studies teachers. A program that does not have a strong partnership with the liberal arts faculty will not receive accreditation, and this is how it should be. In my courses, pre-service teachers are required to complete a "Content and Performance" portfolio. This assignment requires students to take four assignments from their liberal arts classes and develop from them a series of lesson plans. One of the courses must be history; the other three may be from political science, geography, psychology, etc. Students must provide a rationale for why these particular assignments were chosen, and then provide copies of the lessons developed. At the end of the semester, these plans are evaluated by a committee of three: myself (representing the college of education) and two faculty members from liberal arts. Such a partnership increases the rigor of the program and helps students make the necessary connections between their content and their pedagogical work. It also fosters much needed cooperation across campus.

The government is also now more involved in making history the priority that it should be. The *Teaching American History Grant Program* is funded under Title II-C, Subpart 4 of the Elementary and Secondary Education Act. This program's purpose is "to promote the teaching of traditional American history in elementary and secondary schools as a separate academic subject. Grants are used to improve the quality of history instruction by supporting professional development for teachers of American history."[62] These grants provide the needed funds to begin reforming the way social studies is taught.

On July 23, 2004, Tennessee Senator Lamar Alexander introduced a bill cosponsored by Senator Edward M. Kennedy of Massachusetts called the "American History Achievement Act." Alexander decried the poor state of history education in America, and urged his colleagues to join him in doing something about it. Alexander said, "Our children don't know American history because they are not being taught it. For example, the state of Florida recently passed a bill permitting high school students to graduate without taking a course in U.S. history."[63] Later that summer the National Council for History Education urged the Congress to act on the bill and to go even further in improving the state of history education in America.

Pattern A

Grade	Course
7	Regional and Neighborhood History and Geography
8	U.S. History and Geography
9	History of Western Civilization
10	World History and Geography
11	U.S. History and Geography
12	American Government; Social Studies elective

Pattern B

Grade	Course
7	Social Studies elective; Local History
8	U.S. History and Geography
9	World and Western History to 1789
10	World and Western History since 1789
11	U.S. History and Geography
12	American Government; Social Studies elective

Pattern C

Grade	Course
7	World History and Geography to 1789
8	U.S. History and Geography to 1914
9	Social Studies electives
10	World History, Culture, and Geography since 1789
11	U.S. History and Geography, 20th Century
12	American Government; Social Studies elective

Pattern D

Grade	Course
7	Social Studies electives; Local History
8	History of European Civilization
9	History of Non-European Civilizations
10	U.S. History and Geography to 1865
11	U.S. History and Geography since 1865
12	American Government; Social Studies elective

Progress has been made, but there is still much to be done. In 1824, James G. Carter summed up the difficulty in curriculum reform when he noted, "principles of instruction are well guarded against all innovation, even if it should be an improvement."[65] In social studies this has meant that a poorly designed system developed in the still-formative days of the discipline has been carried on to the present day. The attempt to make history into social studies has had the unfortunate effect of muddying the curricular water. Although the resistance to change is an imposing obstacle, social studies reformers need not create a new curriculum out of whole cloth. In fact, the model needed is already in existence.

In 1859 an English philosopher named Herbert Spencer wrote an essay entitled "What Knowledge is of Most Worth?"[66] This essay revolutionized the emerging field of curriculum development, and its seemingly simple question is at the heart of any reform of the social studies that is to be truly successful. It is time to end the attempts to please every social scientist and cover every curricular base. It is time to place the skills and the knowledge gleaned from historical study back at the forefront of a student's curriculum.

Oliver Wendell Holmes said that "As life is action and passion, it is required of a man that he should share the passion and action of his time, at peril of being judged not to have lived." It is imperative that adolescents see the need to share the passion and action of their time, and that they understand the role they will play in the further development of the American ideal. This is the opposite of Jones' vision for social studies, and it must be our total commitment to the young—to the future. Woodrow Wilson said, "I believe in democracy, because it releases the energy of every human being." And I believe in the study of history because, more than any other subject, it prepares every human being to live out this noble sentiment. Philip Zelikow understood the power of history, and he reminded the most powerful man in the world of it. Now we must remind America's young.

---

1 Michael Isikoff, with Daniel Klaidman and Tamara Lipper, "A New Window on the War Room." *Newsweek* (April 12, 2004), 36.
2 Ibid.
3 Ibid.
4 Dynneson and Gross, *Designing Effective Instruction*, 36.
5 Ibid.
6 Ibid.
7 Daniel Tanner and Laurel Tanner, *Curriculum Development: Theory into Practice* (Upper Saddle River, New Jersey: Merrill, 1995), 108.
8 Ibid, 108-110.
9 Dynneson and Gross, 39.
10 Karl Marx and Friedrich Engels, *The Communist Manifesto* (New York: Signet Classic, 1998), 49.
11 Barbara Barksdale Clowse, *Brainpower for the Cold War: The Sputnik Crisis and National Defense Act of 1958* (Westport, Conn.: Greenwood Press, 1981), 7.

12 Kenneth T. Jackson et al., *Building a History Curriculum: Guidelines for Teaching History in Schools* Westlake, OH: National Council for History Education, Inc., 2003), 1.
13 Ibid.
14 Ibid, 5.
15 Ibid, 2.
16 Ibid.
17 Ibid, 1.
18 Ibid.
19 Dewey, *Democracy*, 208.
20 Jackson et al., *Building a History Curriculum*, 2.
21 Laughlin and Hartoonian, *Challenges of Social Studies Instruction*, 16.
22 Ibid, 19.
23 Dewey, 214.
24 Tanner and Tanner, 421.
25 U.S. Department of Education, National Center for Education Statistics, *America's Teachers: Profile of a Profession, 1993-94*, NCES 97-460, by Robin R. Henke, Susan P. Choy, Xianglei Chen, Sonya Geis, Martha Naomi Alt, Stephen P. Broughman, Project Officer. Washington, D.C.: 1997, 23.
26 Ibid, 23-24.
27 Ibid, 24.
28 Jackson et al., Building a History Curriculum, 2-3.
29 Ibid.
30 Ibid, 26.
31 NCES study.
32 NCES study.
33 Ibid, 12.
34 Ibid, 13.
35 http://nces.ed.gov/nationsreportcard/ushistory/whatmeasure.asp
36 Ibid.
37 Ibid.
38 Ravitch, "Who Prepares Our History Teachers?"
39 http://nces.ed.gov/nationsreportcard/ushistory/results/natachieve-g12.asp
40 Ibid.
41 http://nces.ed.gov/nationsreportcard/ushistory/results/natachieve-g4.asp
42 http://nces.ed.gov/nationsreportcard/ushistory/results/natachieve-g8.asp
43 Ravitch.
44 http://nces.ed.gov/nationsreportcard/ushistory/itemmapgr4.asp
45 Jackson, et al., *Building a History Curriculum*, 5.
46 Ibid.
47 Gary Hart, *Restoration of the Republic: The Jeffersonian Ideal in 21st Century America* (Oxford: Oxford University Press, 2002), 3.
48 Jackson et al., *Building a History Curriculum*, 7-8.
49 Ibid, 25.
50 Ibid.
51 Ibid, 16.
52 Richard G. Boehm et al., *States and Regions* (New York: Harcourt Brace and Company, 2000), 18.
53 Ibid, 19.
54 Jackson et al., *Building a History Curriculum*, 16.

55 Mary Beth Klee, "Are They Too Young for History?" *History Matters!* 17 No.4 (December 2004), 1.
56 Jackson et al., *Building a History Curriculum*, 16.
57 Ibid, 17.
58 Ibid, 18.
59 Ibid, 19.
60 Ibid.
61 Ibid.
62 http://www.ed.gov/programs/teachinghistory/index.html
63 http://alexander.senate.gov/news/205822.html
64 Ibid, 20-21.
65 Tanner and Tanner, Curriculum Development, 4.
66 Ibid, 37.

Chapter Three
The Shadow of Colonel Tibbets

It is not at all difficult to understand why, as 1995 dawned in America, retired Brigadier General Paul W. Tibbets, Jr. had a certain expectation that he was going to be feted like royalty by a grateful and honored nation. Tibbets had been a colonel and in command of the 509th Composite Group during World War Two and, everyone agreed, had served his country diligently and honorably; indeed, Colonel Tibbets had played a pivotal role in the ending of the war in the Pacific. So as the fiftieth anniversary of the ending of World War Two approached, Tibbets must have believed that his country would finally get around to placing his name where it rightly belonged: in the pantheon of America's military heroes—right up there with Patton, MacArthur and even Eisenhower.

In August 1945 Paul Tibbets was a 30-year-old pilot with nearly two thousand men under his direct command. Stationed on the island of Tinian, Tibbets was the pilot of a massive B-29 Superfortress—"the most powerful plane ever built."[1] He had joined the military over the objections of his father, but with the support of his mother. In a sign of respect for his mother's "deeply appreciated support" and to "honor her role in his life," Tibbets had named his plane after her—the Enola Gay.[2] On the morning of August 6th Tibbets and his crew took off towards Japan. At 8:15 a.m. the Enola Gay dropped its cargo onto the unsuspecting city of Hiroshima. The bomb included scrawled messages such as, "Greetings to the Emperor from the men of the *Indianapolis*" and had been nicknamed "Little Boy." When it detonated, it created "an instant fireball of several hundred thousand degrees centigrade."[3] "Little Boy" wreaked a kind of hellish havoc the likes of which the world had never before seen. A second bomb, "Fat Man," was dropped on Nagasaki on August 9th.

The successful completion of Tibbets' mission brought to life a horrific scenario that had previously been confined to the pages of science fiction novels and comic books—but it also meant that the seemingly endless carnage of World War Two was drawn to a dramatic close with the unleashing of America's newly acquired power. The GIs were coming home and the limitless parade of flag-draped coffins was drawn to a close. The ingredients for immediate hagiography were all in place, and yet something strange happened on the way to the deification. Tibbets and his crew did not fly off into some glorious sunset.

If the commitment of memory to celluloid may be used as any indication, America's feelings about Tibbets and the Enola Gay have almost always been conflicted. Sergeant Alvin York, the Tennessee farm-boy turned hero/icon of World War One was immortalized by Gary Cooper, and Audie Murphey immortalized himself and his heroics in the European theatre of World War Two in the film *To Hell and Back*. But the film made about Tibbets and his historic flight, *Above and Beyond*, was less celebratory and never became the classic those first two films were. Unlike *Sergeant York* and Murphey's film, *Above and Beyond* does not get aired on national television every Memorial Day or Veteran's Day. There is something vaguely uncertain about its portrayal. Tom Engelhardt describes the mood of the film as "riddled with anxiety" and includes a piece of dialogue spoken by actor Robert Taylor during his portrayal of Colonel Tibbets. "'I think mostly I'm scared for my sons, for their world,' the eternally tense movie Tibbets says in a letter to his mother the night before the mission. 'I'm scared of what can happen if this thing we're unleashing tomorrow doesn't stop this war and all others.'"[4]

Hollywood's dialogue hardly jibes with the embittered certainty Tibbets displayed as the fiftieth anniversary of Hiroshima devolved into bitter controversy. Tibbets' plane had been restored to all its shiny former glory and was to be the centerpiece of an exhibit commemorating the end of the war at the Smithsonian's National Air and Space Museum. It quickly became apparent, however, that trying to mount such an exhibit was fraught with both political and cultural obstacles. Historians who sought to provide an analytical and objective view of the Enola Gay, its legacy and meaning, soon found themselves doing battle with right-wing politicians, veterans' groups and talking heads from the cultural right.

Understandably Paul Tibbets, caught in the middle of this maelstrom, was angered. In his mind, there was nothing controversial about his service. He told an interviewer in June 1994 "that few, if any of the articles, books, films or reports have ever attempted to discuss the missions of August 6th and August 9th in the context of the times. Simply stated, the Enola Gay and the 509th Composite Bomb Group have been denied a historically correct representation to the public. Most writers have looked to the ashes of Hiroshima and Nagasaki to find answers for the use of those atomic weapons. The real answers lay in thousands of graves from Pearl Harbor around the world to Normandy and back again."[5] Tibbets believed that his story was a relatively simple one: the Japanese were our enemy, we were at war, and his actions brought the war to a close. America's victory had not been a desultory one; it had been the result of sacrifice and heroism and it was a story that needed and deserved to be told in properly reverential tones. Historians and academics who wanted to talk about the savagery of the aftermath of Hiroshima and Nagasaki were missing the point or, more insidiously, trying to tarnish America's victory. Tom Crouch, who was the museum's chairman of the Aeronautics Department, seemed to have been presciently concerned about this possible conflict when he wrote museum director Martin Harwit and asked, "Do you want to do an exhibition intended to make veterans feel good, or do you want an exhibition that will lead our visitors to think about the consequences of the atomic bombing of Japan? Frankly, I don't think we can do both."[6]

The controversy over the National Air and Space Museum's proposed Enola Gay exhibit would reach a boiling point that would lead to a complete capitulation by the museum's directors. Under threat from reactionaries in Congress to gut its funding, director Harwit resigned and the exhibition that was eventually unveiled was a shadow of its former self, redrawn to assure that no one would be offended. The end of World War Two also brought the birth of the Atomic Age with all of its neuroses, fears, and doubts, but this side of the story was now officially taboo, and anyone who dared to speak of it was dishonoring America and her veterans. Tibbets and the Enola Gay would be spared historical criticism in the mainstream, but would also be confined to what may be an even worse fate—historical irrelevance. It has become an unspoken rule in American history classrooms that subjects which are controversial must be glossed over or, preferably, ignored. And so it was. When the sixtieth anniversary of the Enola Gay's mission rolled around in August 2005 there was barely a peep in the press or the academic community. A 90-year-old Tibbets, in deteriorating health and living in Ohio, must have wondered about this second Pyrrhic victory.

For most Americans, the entire controversy of 1995 must have been truly shocking. After all, the way in which most of us have been taught history has never left room for interpretation. There was always a clear ending, and the good guys and bad guys were always obvious and easily delineated. How could there be controversy when the answers were always so damn simple? America had always been marching inexorably towards a brighter tomorrow, always progressing towards a more perfect union, with freedom and justice for all. That was the narrative to which young Americans became accustomed and to which older Americans clung ever more tenaciously as evil left-wing professor types chipped away at the myths. We were (and are) a heroic people from sea to shining sea. What in the world was there to debate? As John W. Dover has so succinctly phrased it, "Heroic narratives demand a simple, unilinear story line."[7] Any deviation from this story line is labeled "revisionist" and quickly shunted aside before the innocent minds of our young people are blemished with liberal fancies of historical complexity and multi-layered notions of *truth*. The result of teaching history this way is not merely a jingoistic patriotic soup, but one of the most boring concoctions one generation has ever dared to foist upon another: social studies. James W. Loewen points out that "history is the only field in which the more courses students take, the stupider they become."[8]

When we remove the controversy and the drama from the teaching of history what we are left with is an amalgam of dates and meaningless factoids to be rehearsed and regurgitated. Alfred North Whitehead has written that the "diplomatic and political stuff with which we cram children is a very thin view of history."[9] This thin view is particularly troubling since history is nothing more and nothing less than the story of mankind's triumphs and struggles, and it should be obvious that such a subject is naturally filled with tension, drama, romance and all sorts of intrigue. But something gets lost in the translation, because the material presented to students across this nation year after year is devoid of drama. Loewen places much of the blame for this on the vanilla textbooks that are available for history teachers. He writes:

> The stories that history textbooks tell are predictable; every problem has already been solved or is about to be solved. Textbooks exclude conflict or real suspense. They leave out anything that might reflect badly upon our national character. When they try for drama, they achieve only melodrama, because readers know that everything will turn out fine in the end. 'Despite setbacks, the United States overcame these challenges,' in the words of one textbook. Most authors of history textbooks don't even try for melodrama. Instead, they write in a tone that if heard aloud might be described as 'mumbling lecturer.' No wonder students lost interest.[10]

But students do more than simply lose interest in the subject of history—they lose interest in the practice of democracy. Even the white-hot bitterness and vitriol of the 2004 presidential campaign between George W. Bush and John F. Kerry was not enough to motivate young Americans to head to the polls. Only fifty-eight percent of voters 18-24 years old were even registered to vote, and of these less than half (forty-seven percent) bothered to actually vote.[11] And why should they? Their history courses had no doubt engrained in them the belief that America just somehow always gets the leaders she needs and things, as Loewen states, always "turn out fine in the end."

This situation requires that educators radically rethink the way that we teach history. We must move away from the dry, traditional way in which it has been taught. There is no (or, at least, there should be no) equivalent in the study of history and the pursuit of historical "truth" to the spelling and grammar bees that have become standard fare for the study of the English language. In order to prepare students for active societal involvement in a democracy, students must be given the opportunity to put the passive knowledge of facts into the action of critical thinking. The ultimate goal of social studies, then, is not the ability to regurgitate facts on a subjective test, but to interpret fact in some form, whether it is some type of testing or in the composition of a research or synthesis paper.

Such a change will not come easily. The reliance on memorization and "correct" simple answers is a longstanding characteristic of social studies. Part of the reason for this is simple survival. Teachers have learned to impose a kind of "self-censorship" upon themselves in order to avoid falling into the kind of controversial quagmire that occurred over the Smithsonian's Enola Gay exhibit.[12] The development of critical thinking skills in students "requires that students learn to investigate issues using all pertinent evidence, to suspend judgment until all the pertinent evidence is brought to near on the issues, to test hypotheses, to discriminate fact from opinion, and so on. A free society requires this."[13] But the family is often not a "free society" and this type of examination may well—indeed, hopefully will—lead students to question some of the "truths" they have been taught at home. Too often this kind of curriculum is reflexively labeled "revisionist" and ended because of its controversial nature.

I recently asked a group of teachers who are working on their Master's degree in education to provide me with a description of the school system. The one word answer that I heard from the entire group was, "Fear." *Fear*, they said in unanimity, is running our schools. Teachers are afraid of parents, students and administrators. Administrators are afraid of everything, but primarily they are afraid of being sued. We live in an age where if one dares to say anything of substance at all, someone from some group or some side of the political spectrum will be offended. Many history teachers have responded to this ugly climate by saying and asking nothing of substance. The result is a curriculum based on trying to please everyone and to avoid, at all costs, the dreaded label of *revisionist*. Of course the very notion of revision in historical inquiry is intellectually vacuous, because it implies a static, universally-agreed-upon interpretation of the past. This is something that has simply never existed, and therefore being a revisionist is purely redundant to being a historian. If a history curriculum is to have any relevance or interest for our students, then we must encourage the kind of free-ranging inquiry that often brings about controversy.

This intellectual battle for the soul of history is not new, of course. As we have seen with the Hampton Method, it has long been understood that the way we teach history has an impact on the kinds of citizens we get, and therefore this battle is vested with great import. In the 1880s the Memoriter System gained prominence in American schools. This system "relied on the use of a textbook from which students were expected to reproduce the exact words of the text."[14] Clearly, then, under this system there was no premium placed on critical thinking. Rather, the textbook and, to a lesser degree the history teacher, was set aside as an expert. Questioning would have been futile in this setting because the textbook offered, as textbooks so often do, the only interpretation and the only "correct" answer. Consequently, if the text referred to Lincoln as "the Great Emancipator," then that is exactly who he was. There was no need for discussion or analysis. This marvelous system gave rise to the American phenomenon of adults who could recite the preamble to the United States Constitution but who could not tell you what those words meant in practical application to their lives. The impetus to create loyal citizens led to creating only mindless mimics who were able to spout the party line. This is most assuredly not the purpose of historical study and consciousness.

This system had its critics then as now. In 1883, noted teacher educator Mary Sheldon Barnes "was scathingly critical of the Memoriter System and offered—as an alternative to the imparting of information—curriculum aimed at awakening a spirit of inquiry."[15] Barnes sought to encourage critical thinking skills in history. She suggested three types of questions that could be formulated in such a way as to facilitate this process. First, she asked for the use of analytical questions. These questions, she argued, would allow students to search for the valuable historical material on their own, rather than being spoon-fed such material by a textbook. Second, Ms. Barnes offered the use of "synthetic" questions. These were designed to get students to "draw the information together into a coherent image of the past society." Finally, she suggested the use of evaluative questions "that asked students to reflect on the ideals, character, and moral qualities of the historical personages and society."[16] Having students pass moral judgments on their ancestors and the world of their ancestors is ripe for the kind of controversy that dogged Martin Hewit and the Smithsonian. That may well be the reason that social studies reformers are still, to this day, making the same sort of recommendations for the improvement of the curriculum that Mary Sheldon Barnes made over a century ago.

The challenge, then, is to return the drama to the telling and studying of history and, perhaps more to the point, to allow students' opinions to coalesce and be given voice within our classrooms. This is not a challenge that will be met easily, however. Allowing American students to think about and even question this nation's history has some powerful opponents. Maintaining the status quo in the teaching of history is, as those at the Hampton Institute understood so well, a unique tool in maintaining the status quo in the nation's political and economic status quo. Theologian Reinhold Neibuhr has written that:

> The physical sciences gained their freedom when they overcame the traditionalism based on ignorance, but the traditionalism which the social sciences face is based upon the economic interest of the dominant social classes who are trying to maintain their special privileges in society.[17]

Questioning the dominant stories and mythologies of the past may well lead to the questioning of the present—an outcome that many if not most of America's elite find disturbing to say the least.

A second obstacle is the students themselves. The great classicist Edith Hamilton bluntly stated that, "People hate being made to think, above all upon fundamental problems."[18] And yet get our students to think we must, because this ability is all that may stand between the preservation of our democracy and the abyss. The tragedy of traditional American education is that it prepares students to accept uncritically rather than to think and question everything. This dichotomy is not lost on the young. They recognize that we use

> ...autocratic schools...for teaching students to be responsible citizens in a democratic society. Ironically, the first experience most students have with government is when their state's compulsory education laws require them to attend school. They are forced into a system of rules and decisions not unlike the authority they encounter at home, an authority that rewards obedience, punishes offenders, and needs no justification other than 'I am the authority here.'[19]

Such disgraceful hypocrisy belittles the meaning of education and does irreparable damage to the practice of freedom. In our current school system and in the modern mode of "teaching" history, students are not enabled in the pursuit of truth or encouraged to think for themselves. The result is a frightening inclination to simply go along, to feel disenfranchised long before they have made even the most cursory attempt at contributing to their community or their society.

We may look to the former Soviet Union for an example of ways in which the study of history may be reclaimed from petty nationalism and reinvigorated for future generations. A survey conducted by Germany's Koerber Institute found that Russian students believed that the study of history was relevant "as a means of social orientation" and that they disagreed with the notion that history was a "useless and distasteful topic."[20] Their attitude was notably more positive than their peers in England and other areas of Europe. Tatyana Volodina, a professor at Tula State Pedagogical University, credits this positive attitude towards history in Russia to a new, more open and less dogmatic approach to history since the fall of the Soviet Union.

The collapse of communism and the Soviet Union forced a sudden and often harsh re-evaluation of the study and teaching of history in Russia. One Russian historian said that "it is immoral for young people to take exams" on information taught from Soviet-era textbooks. "I can give you my assurance," he went on, "that there is not a single page without a falsification."[21] As the totalitarian regime of the communists fell, many former students became bitter as their own cherished myths were looked at anew. One teacher told of a confrontation with a former student in which the student exclaimed, "I would hang you...and all the history teachers too! You painted a fairy-tale about a bright future and now we have to pay for that."[22] But with the bitterness came a piqued interest. Volodina writes that "students accused their teachers of lies, but at the same time they wanted to devour new historical knowledge."[23]

What, exactly, this new historical knowledge would look like was very much up for grabs in the years immediately following the demise of communism. One possibility was a history which held that Russia had a violent and "bad" past that needed to be overcome by succeeding generations. This new history was a reaction to the oppression of scholarly freedom under communist rule. "The new history textbooks that appeared in Russian schools in the mid-1990s had a reproachful, anti-communist tone" writes Volodina.[24] These texts gave students the clear impression that "every nation gets the government it deserves" and produced "feelings of national inferiority."[25]

The Soros Foundation was one of many private entities that secured authorization by Russia's Ministry of Education to publish history textbooks for Russia's school children. The Soros books were characterized by a pronounced pro-Western bias and a certain degree of condescension towards the Russian people and their past. A Soros Foundation textbook published for fifth graders, for example, taught that in the eighteenth century "nobody would do anything without an order in Russia" and "Russian serfs did not try to work hard, while western laborers worked hard because they knew that the harder they worked the more they would earn."[26] One such text, written by Alexander Kreder, caused particular consternation in Russia. Volodina writes that "...the older generation [of Russians] expressed intense hatred for Kreder's book and declared that all defenders of Kreder and Soros were the participants in an anti-Russian Zionist plot."[27]

Clearly these textbooks brought about a serious backlash from the Russian population who, like most Americans, believed that their children deserved a history that would induce civic and national pride, not self-reproach, guilt and shame. A fight erupted in Russia akin to the battle that raged in America regarding national history standards in 1994. That year right-wing talker Rush Limbaugh said:

> ...that the [new US history education] standards were part of the America-bashing multi-cultural agenda that he had cautioned viewers and listeners about. For many months, he had excoriated historians who had 'bullied their way into power positions in academia' in order to indoctrinate students with the message that 'our country is inherently evil.'[28]

Many Russians believed that their own heritage was under attack, and the result, as in America, was a reflexive nationalism. Volodina notes that, "Public opinion swung again in the direction of nationalism, and some leaders reintroduced into political discourse theories of Russia's historical uniqueness as an antidote to the post-Soviet sickness of guilt and humiliation."[29]

In the midst of the Russian-version of our own "culture wars" emerged a refreshing alternative, what President Bill Clinton might have called a historical third way. The result of this forced national introspection and reflection was that Russians discovered what they really desired from historical study was "national self-esteem but also a careful consideration of the past."[30] In a realization that would no doubt stun Rush Limbaugh and his ilk, Russian parents and schoolchildren discovered that it was indeed possible to have both. The quotation below is how Volodina describes the new mode of historical instruction in Russian schools. It is a description that will surely make American history teachers turn deep green with envy. He writes:

> When state history examinations were reinstated, the Ministry of Education published special instructions and sent them to schools. This document affirmed that students may voice opinions that agree with neither the classroom teacher nor the textbook. However, students should support their opinions with facts and arguments. The Ministry also recognized that the best textbooks invite teachers and students to develop their historical thinking abilities. Books like these encourage students to wrap their minds around difficult analytical questions...Students are encouraged to address historical problems, and the best textbooks do not give them ready answers...Therefore, students get an opportunity to argue about and interpret facts, not trusting any authorities, verdicts or opinions.[31]

Living in a totalitarian state for decades clearly taught Russian policy makers and educators the importance of the ability to *think critically* about the historical past. It is a lesson Americans have yet to learn.

Thus we face the daunting question: how do we get there from here? How do we teach history in a way that will empower children and young adults and prepare them to take their place as leaders in our country? How do educators insure that our students are given "an opportunity to argue about and interpret facts, not trusting any authorities, verdicts or opinions?" At the very real risk of sounding naively idealistic or woefully simplistic I will posit one very blunt proposal: the reform of the teaching of history in America begins with the utilization of a constructivist teaching philosophy within our history classrooms. Teaching history from a constructivist outlook means that we must place at the center of our curriculum the notion that students are capable of forming their own valid opinions and we must make *thought* our most cherished outcome. It means that we incorporate the radical notion into our classrooms that our students have thoughts worthy of our respect. A constructivist classroom will move away from the time-honored but useless practice of pretending that history is a subject about which there are no controversies and that is made up of facts about which there is no disagreement. Our students know better.

An example of a student knowing better than the pabulum he was consistently offered in his social studies curriculum recently came to my attention. One of my pre-service social studies teachers was placed into a second grade classroom in a small, rural school in western North Carolina. She struggled because of her cooperating teacher's incredible desire to avoid the discussion of absolutely anything that might cause any form of even slight controversy. My student broached the idea of having students write letters to soldiers serving in Iraq. Oh, no, she was told, we don't even talk about Iraq in this classroom. Some of the parents might not like it. Later, my student asked about having the second graders write letters of support or collect canned goods for the children affected by the near-biblical devastation caused to the city of New Orleans by Hurricane Katrina. Oh, no, she was told, we're not going to talk about the hurricane in this class because it might upset some of the children. This poor student teacher was quite ready to throw her hands up and resign herself to a semester's worth of fluff.

Then one day she taught a lesson on the pledge of allegiance. I have my pre-service elementary school social studies teachers read James Clavell's *The Children's Story* and think about what it means. Often, my students read the book—which describes the power teachers have to mold young minds and the inherent dangers of such power—and describe it as "spooky," "eerie," or "disturbing." They are always frustrated (and I am always depressed) by the fact that, when quizzed, they know nothing about the pledge's history. They are embarrassed (though this emotion rightly belongs to their teachers and not to them) when they find that they have been pledging allegiance and mouthing words they don't understand—the vast majority of these students, semester after semester, cannot accurately define a "republic." Inspired by this knowledge, this student taught these second graders about the pledge. She even dared to tell them that "under God" had been added because of the Cold War in an effort to distinguish America from the Godless communists.

The lesson was a success—even the timid cooperating teacher liked it. After the lesson, one of the second graders—one of those same sheltered, protected- from-all-historical-nastiness students—came up to her and asked a question. He liked the lesson, he said, but wanted to know something: could she tell him anything about that *other* flag? You know, he said, the one with the stars in an "x" on both sides? *You know*, he said, *the one we're supposed to be ashamed of and not use, but my parents fly in our yard anyway*? I was reminded of Dewey writing that "The true starting point of history is always some present situation with its problems."[32] This child didn't need to be protected from the often uncomfortable difficulties of history—he no doubt had a better inherent understanding of them than his spineless teacher.

The use of constructivism, we must hope, will allow for more student input and will, hopefully, do away with this banal belief that we can shelter coming generations from the chilly winds of history. It will also help to increase the level of civic competency—one of the original goals of the formation of the social studies curriculum. Constructivism will move our social studies classrooms away from the droll monotony of rote memorization and recitation of facts and will drive the curriculum towards a more in-depth understanding and ability on the part of students to interpret and make most use of historical information. This is not merely a shift in pedagogy; it is a total reformation of the goals and methods of historical instruction and understanding. "Were all instructors to realize that the quality of mental process, not the production of correct answers, is the measure of educative growth," Dewey wrote, "something hardly less than a revolution in teaching would be worked."[33]

As it relates to the individual teacher, constructivism has been defined as a philosophy in which "the teacher creates, or constructs, her own approach to teaching by considering personal experience, alternative instructional approaches, the unique features of the individual classroom, formal learning theories, and various philosophies of education."[34] The key elements to this idea are that knowledge will be constructed and that proper use will be made of the life experiences of the educator. From the students' perspective, constructivism is defined as "a child-centered approach that focuses on knowledge construction, not knowledge reproduction. Constructivism emphasizes that students interpret new objects and events by trying to alter or modify existing mental structures that had formed as a result of their previous life experiences."[35]

So what do these definitions mean in practice? Postman and Weingartner point out that:

> ...one of the tenets of a democratic society is that men be allowed to think and express themselves freely on any subject, even to the point of speaking out against the idea of a democratic society. To the extent that our schools are instruments of such a society, they must develop in the young not only an aware-

ness of this freedom but a will to exercise it, and the intellectual power and perspectives to do so effectively.[36]

In social studies, constructivism means nothing less than training students to carefully and critically examine the beloved tales and, in many cases *myths*, of American history. The construction of knowledge, as it applies to history, means that students will no longer be handed the "right" or "correct" answers in their formulation of an historical understanding. Common sense, so often in short supply in the business of curriculum development, tells us that any true study of history does not lend itself to dogmatic interpretations of the material. For instance, while two plus two will always equal four, there is general and passionate disagreement about such diverse historical topics as why we fought the second world war, whether or not Abraham Lincoln is truly deserving of the moniker "The Great Emancipator," and who was the greatest (in this instance meaning the most effective) United States president. These answers call for opinions—not concrete, rote responses. Loewen writes that, "To succeed, schools must help us learn how to ask questions about our society and its history and how to figure out answers for ourselves."[37]

Perhaps the best definition of constructivism that I have read comes from Russian dramatist Constantin Stanislavski. He described the progression that an actor would make as a result of growth in their vocation. Stanislavski wrote, "Gradually you will become adept in sorting out your impressions of a new play. You will learn how to reject what is untrue, excessive, unimportant, how to discover what is fundamental, how to listen to others and to yourself, *and how to find your own way amid the opinions of others* [italics added]."[38] This ability is what Postman and Weingartner call a "crap detector."[39] Such ability is vital in a democratic society and should be the cornerstone of why we choose to teach social studies. Education must, after all, be relevant to be successful. If we are engaged in a curriculum that does not offer young people the chance to think and to practice dissecting the arguments and opinions of others, then there really is no good answer to the old question, "Why do we need to learn this?"

Our answer to this question, at least in social studies, should be because democracy is fragile and our freedoms are, always have been, and always will be tenuous. Dewey has written that "The only freedom that is of enduring importance is freedom of intelligence, that is to say, freedom of observation and of judgment exercised in behalf of purposes that are intrinsically worth while."[40] If education is fundamentally about providing students with a crap detector, then let's get about the business of providing it, because there is a great deal of crap to be detected these days—in the halls of Congress, in boardrooms across the nation, at City Hall, and no doubt in our homes. Instead, we continue to march in step with the old philosophy of the Hampton Method, denying our students the freedom of intelligence they so desperately crave, need and deserve. The results are all around us—a democracy that seems to be less democratic by the day and a populace that seems less interested in their government and the issues of the day than with who will win the latest reality television contest. Polls show that Americans continue to trust their government less and less, but we all seem to feel powerless to confront that same government. The distinctly American notion that power resides in the people—with the governed instead of the government—continues to slip away because too many American children have never been taught the simple but profound truth that in this country thinking is a right and a responsibility that must be practiced and for which we should all be willing and ready to fight. "On the other hand," writes Forrest Gathercoal, "autocratic classrooms do no recognize rights, but think in terms of 'student privileges,' *usually equating responsibility with obedience* [italics added]."[41]

Orwell wrote that those who controlled the past controlled the present, and that is still true today. By refusing to allow our students to form and defend their own opinions, we deny them the very practice of democracy. Our current way of teaching is deeply autocratic and allows, indeed *demands*, the total passivity of students. The study, indeed the burden of history plays a direct role in this mindless form of "education." We need their butts in the seats for funding, but we seem to care precious little about whether or not their minds follow. In fact, the more passive and docile our students are in the social studies classroom the less likely we will stumble accidentally into some controversy. Desperately hoping to avoid any Martin Harwit-like trouble, the texts and the myths are parroted over and over until our students know them but care positively nothing about them.

Great care must be taken in the incorporation of constructivist pedagogy, however. Constructivism, like progressive education before, is often harmed as much by its practitioners as its detractors. Placing such emphasis on the thoughts of students, on their construction of knowledge and opinions, does not mean that we are to do away with the primacy of facts in the acquiring of such skills and dispositions. While rote memorization is tedious and uneducative, there can be no construction of *valid* opinions without first a mastery of the facts involved (the popularity of Bill O'Reilly not withstanding).

As Dewey said in defending progressive education, "Just because traditional education was a matter of routine in which the plans and programs were handed down from the past, it does not follow that progressive education is a matter of planless improvisation."[42]

To be sure, my call for a constructivist approach in our study of history is not an argument for the abandonment of facts. Rather, history teachers must understand that the transmission of facts is only the *beginning* in the study of history. Sadly, the study of history only really begins in the margins that educators have marked off as the endpoints, the places where standardized tests are brought in and final assessments made. We have mistaken the tools for the product. As Dewey says, "The past just as past is no longer our affair. If it were wholly gone and done with, there would be only one reasonable attitude toward it. Let the dead bury their dead. But knowledge of the past is the key to understanding the present."[43] Think of that North Carolina second grader, whose questioning about the Confederate flag and the concomitant emotions it arouses so powerfully illustrates the converging of the past and the present, yesterday and today. Constructivism forces educators to allow students to make use of facts, to move away from what Whitehead so contemptuously referred to as inert ideas (Whitehead went so far as to proclaim, "A merely well-informed man is the most useless bore on God's earth.").[44]

To ask students to construct their own view of history is no small task. This cannot be done without a firm grounding—a solid foundation—in the facts and figures of history. So we must guard against placing the proverbial cart before the horse. We should not ask students to interpret that with which they are not familiar. A student cannot assess the presidency of Ronald Reagan without first having a factual grasp of the Reagan era. Otherwise, what we get from students will be little more than the parroting of the political views espoused at home or a mirror-image of Clavell's classroom. Neither of these will suffice to make good citizens. The facts come first. There is no romantic way of phrasing this proposition, but neither is one required. A certain amount of "leg work" is due before we can accomplish the critical thinking that we desire. As Lev Vygotsky wrote, we may be assured that "there is no such thing as play without rules."[45] Simply put, students cannot think critically unless they have adequate material and information about which to think.

Whitehead has already provided us with the necessary framework for making constructivism a powerful reality within our approach to history education. Better than any other theorist before or since, Whitehead points out the place of freedom and discipline and refuses to allow educators to be forced into a false choice between the two. "The antithesis in education," he wrote, "between freedom and discipline is not so sharp as a logical analysis of the meanings of the terms might lead us to imagine."[46] His "rhythms of education"—expounded in his book *The Aims of Education*—are a constructivist model that may be used in our classrooms. In Whitehead's classic formulation, we must first capture our students' interest, then provide them with the factual material of our subject matter and, finally, let them loose to evaluate, question and struggle with this material. He labels these three stages as *romance*, *precision*, and *generalization*. From this process the construction of meaning and knowledge will occur.

Whether history teachers like it or not, before we can offer our students freedom or discipline, we must first get their attention; we must compete with popular culture, hormones, and society to convince our students that our subject matter is worthy of their time. "Because I said so" is not a valid reason, and neither is "Because it will be on the end-of-grade test the government forces me to administer." Whitehead tells us that "There can be no mental development without interest. Interest is the *sine qua non* for attention and apprehension...without interest there will be no progress."[47] How do we command our student' interest? Whitehead urges us to use romance—to entice the student with wonder. Nancy A. Hewitt, a professor of History and Women's Studies at Rutgers University says that students "love to learn more about the personal lives of famous people, especially material that makes them seem more like real individuals with families, problems, challenges, etc."[48] Hewitt points out that a history that consists of ordinary humans accomplishing extraordinary things is more likely to attract and hold attention than our traditional way of teaching, which seems to show that god-like men appear on the scene at just the right moment to save the nation. These minor deities hold nothing to which our students can relate. "One fact that never fails to amaze [the students]," Hewitt continues, "is that Pocahontas was only twelve or thirteen years old when she 'saved' John Smith. When I try to get them to think about the implications of that fact, of her position in Powhatan society, as one of Chief Powhatan's several daughters, they begin to see the differences between myth and history."[49] Such a distinction is useful as a way of showing students the practical applications of historical inquiry—that it can provide them with a crap detector.

Gaining their attention is not enough, of course. Once we have it, we must do something with it—something worthwhile. This is the crucial phase that Whitehead has labeled as "precision." This stage "is dominated by the fact that there are right ways and wrong ways, and definite truths to be known" says Whitehead.[50] This stage helps us to rescue constructivism from those who have turned it into the educational equivalent of moral relativism—where the opinion is valued even when it cannot be supported with facts because we dare not harm the student's precious self-esteem. Such pandering is not worthy of the name of education, but it has a mighty hold on too many classrooms and far too many teacher-preparation programs. "An unskillful practioner," Whitehead warns, "can easily damage a sensitive organism."[51] Such has often been the case with constructivism.

I find that many teachers are afraid of the stage of precision because they have been trained out of their own good instincts by their preparation programs. They know, as we all do on some level, that there are, indeed, *correct ways* of doing certain things. There are correct ways to research and there are correct ways to construct an argument. Here is where we can carry the metaphor forward—if we hold to the tenet that our goal is for our students to construct their own opinions and knowledge rather than being mere passive receptacles for ours or that of the state's, then the tools with which they construct this knowledge are *facts*. Too many so-called constructivists believe that any opinion is valid and that the teacher's job is simply to stay out of the way. It is no wonder, then, that so many behavioralists judge constructivism so harshly. We must remember that facts are to be viewed as neither an anchor nor an albatross. Rather, they should be seen as the platform from which we leap, unfettered by superstition or dogma, into true freedom. An opinion which cannot stand under the scrutiny of facts belongs to the realm of faith—not education.

Richard E. Mayer of the University of California-Santa Barbara has written that there is increasing evidence to show that "cognitive activity rather than behavioral activity, instructional guidance rather than pure discovery, and curricular focus rather than unstructured exploration" is the most effective way of promoting constructivist learning."[52] Mayer criticizes many in the field of education for making *constructivism* synonymous with *hands-on* learning. He is deeply suspicious of learning environments where students "are free to work...with little or no guidance."[53] Constructivists have often made hands-on activities "ends in themselves" when the end should be knowledge.[54] The teacher's role in constructivism is more than that of a glorified baby-sitter. Using Whitehead's formula, we try and spark their interest through the use of romance, and then we help them to discover and interpret facts. Finally, we—the teachers—must be prepared to evaluate the students' evidence and their argument. Those who would make a constructivist teacher stand on the sidelines while students blindly search for truth do not understand the concept or the meaning of constructivism.

Whitehead defends the need for precision by writing:

> There is no getting away from the fact that things have been found out, and that to be effective in the modern world you must have a store of definite acquirement of the best practice. To write poetry you must study metre; and to build bridges you must be learned in the strength of material. Even the Hebrew prophets had to learn to write, probably in those days requiring no mean effort. The untutored art of genius is—in the words of the Prayer Book—a vain thing, fondly invented.[55]

We must train students to absorb and seek facts in order to build sustainable, defensible opinion. This is a great responsibility for any and all teachers. Education is a journey and facts are our means of making this journey. It is the role of the teacher in a constructivist classroom of history to place the facts before the students—not to interpret them for the class—but to provide them with the information. What new opinions and ideals are formed from these facts is the province of nature. But make no mistake, the teacher's role in a constructivist classroom is not diminished and not to be underestimated.

As Mayer points out, there are many studies that show that guided discovery is a more effective tool for teaching than so-called pure discovery (whether it is under the guise of active learning or pure discovery learning or social constructivism). "Although guided discovery required the most learning time," he writes, "it resulted in the best performance on solving transfer problems."[56] Constructivism in the history classroom is about more than coloring maps or making mud adobes or even sitting in discussion groups. The construction of knowledge involves facts and precision, and it is the teacher's job to provide his or her students with these things.

What sort of facts are we talking about in the study of history? Is it merely the study of dates, or the memorization of capitols and geographic features? Have we not already dismissed these as trivial? The answer is yes and no. A student who develops and argues an opinion which states that Abraham Lincoln was a failure as president but cannot place the American Civil War in the correct century would be hard to take seriously. While we must value the process of constructing knowledge and respect the outcomes from the individual student, we do not do so at the expense of intellectual standards or rigor. To do so is to cheat our students and demean our vocation.

The final stage of Whitehead's rhythms of education he has labeled as "generalization." At the stage of romance we have piqued our students' interest, we have gone above and beyond to convince them that the curriculum we have to offer is worth while, interesting, and relevant to them and to their lives; at the stage of precision they have mastered facts and are now armed with details. Now, as Whitehead writes, "The pupil...wants to use his new weapons."[57] We hear all the time from teachers that their great aim—their overriding goal for students—is critical thinking. This is what is meant by the stage of generalization. We now ask our students to *apply* the knowledge they have gathered, to make use of it in a way relevant to their lives and their situation. The students have learned that John F. Kennedy was assassinated; now we ask them to use what they know about him to imagine what a second term might have been like. Would Vietnam have escalated? Would the counter-culture have defined the late 1960s if JFK had lived? Imagine these possibilities, we say, and ground all that you posit in fact. Such exercises flex the mind and make history so much more than the dull tale of a black and white past that currently passes for "social studies."

The application of such knowledge and the articulation of grounded opinions will lead students to an understanding of their role in a democratic society; this will allow our students to be better prepared for the rights and responsibilities of citizenship. Such application is relevant in that it may well inform the remainder of a person's adult life. Looking at things such as the predominant political philosophies of their time, a student must begin to ask him or herself which (if any) best fits with his or her own moral code and personal ethics. Will they work to support a strong or a weak centralized government? Will they toss their hat in with the pro-life or the pro-choice movement? What issues do they feel passionately enough about to make a public stand—even if it brings the disapprobation of their friends and neighbors? Using Whitehead's formula as a guide for applying constructivism in the social studies classroom, we empower students to not only be able to answer the "what" questions of the citizen's life, but also the all important and too often neglected "why" questions. Discovering our own place in society and defining and refining our own beliefs is the first and most valuable step in becoming a citizen.

Although such self-discovery is an important outcome in a constructivist social studies classroom, it will not be the final outcome. Rather, such self-development and fulfillment is but the prerequisite for changing modern social institutions. Thus the constructivist social studies teacher has much more in mind than merely the growth of the individual student. The major objective will be allowing the student, through the application of his or her own individual growth, to contribute in a positive way to society. Cicero taught that to be ignorant of history is to remain a child. In order to prepare our students best for their role as adult contributors to a free nation, we must reform the social studies and apply constructivist principles in our classrooms.

The use of constructivism, particularly as described in Alfred North Whitehead's rhythms of education, gives students ownership of the material, the outcomes, and eventually the use of what they have learned in the broader societal context. There is nothing more important than allowing the young to feel this sense of ownership and empowerment with regards to the story of their nation— the very same nation that some of them will one day lead. As Goethe wrote, "The destiny of a nation, at any given time, depends on the opinions of its young men, under twenty-five."[58] I would of course add the opinions of its young women, as well. Goethe understood, as we must, that the opinions of the young will shape our tomorrow. Giving our students a real say in the interpretation of our nation's past provides them with powerful practice for weighing evidence, forming an opinion, and then skillfully articulating it. The alternative is that "the attitude of the pupil must, upon the whole, be one of docility, receptivity, and obedience," in Dewey's famous phrase.[59] Our own common sense and experience tells us that such a view is not sufficient to attract the attention and inspire the passion of our students. And if this is not our ultimate goal, then perhaps the social studies itself should become history.

---

1 Tom Engelhardt, "The Victors and the Vanquished," in *History Wars: The Enola Gay and other Battles for the American Past*, Eds. Edward T. Linenthal and Tom Engelhardt (New York: Henry Holt and Company, 1996), 229.
2 Ibid, 230.
3 Ibid, 231.
4 Ibid, 232.
5 Ibid, 240.
6 Edward T. Linenthal, "Anatomy of a Controversy," in *History Wars: The Enola Gay and other Battles for the American Past*, Eds. Edward T. Linenthal and Tom Engelhardt (New York: Henry Holt and Company, 1996), 35.
7 John W. Dover, "Three Narratives of Our Humanity," in *History Wars: The Enola Gay and other Battles for the American Past*, eds. Edward T. Linenthal and Tom Engelhardt (New York: Henry Holt and Company, 1996), 80.
8 James W. Loewen, *Lies My Teacher Told Me: Everything Your American History Textbook Got Wrong* (New York: Touchstone Books, 1995), 12.
9 Alfred North Whitehead, *The Aims of Education and Other Essays*, (New York: The Free Press, 1929), 66.
10 Loewen, *Lies*, 13.
11 "U.S. Voter Turnout Up in 2004, Census Bureau Reports," United States Census Bureau Press release, May 26, 2005. Retrieved from www.census.gov/Press-Release/www/releases/archives/voting/004986.htm on September 25, 2005.
12 Tanner and Tanner, *Curriculum Development*, 567-68.
13 Ibid, 568.
14 John D. McNeil, *Curriculum: The Teacher's Initiative*, (Upper Saddle River, New Jersey: Merrill, 1999), 102.
15 Ibid, 103.
16 Ibid.

17 Reinhold Niebuhr, *Moral Man and Immoral Society: A Study in Ethics and Politics*, (Louisville, KY: Westminster John Knox Press, 2001), xxvii.
18 Edith Hamilton, *The Greek Way* (New York: W.W. Norton, 1993), 172.
19 Forrest Gathercoal, *Judicious Discipline*, (San Francisco: Caddo Gap Press, 2004), 75.
20 Tatyana Volodina, "Teaching History in Russia After the Collapse of the USSR," *The History Teacher* 38, no.2 (February 2005), 179-180.
21 Ibid, 181.
22 Ibid.
23 Ibid.
24 Ibid, 182.
25 Ibid.
26 Ibid, 183.
27 Ibid.
28 Gary B. Nash, Charlotte Crabtree and Ross E. Dunn, *History on Trial: Culture Wars and the Teaching of the Past* (New York: Vintage Books, 2000), 5.
29 Volodina, "Teaching History in Russia," 183.
30 Ibid, 184.
31 Ibid.
32 John Dewey, *Democracy and Education*, (New York: The Free Press, 1944), 214.
33 Ibid, 176.
34 David G. Armstrong and Tom V. Savage, *Teaching in the Secondary School, An Introduction*, (Upper Saddle River, New Jersey: Merrill, 1998), 70.
35 George W. Maxim, *Dynamic Social Studies for Constructivist Classrooms: Inspiring Tomorrow's Social Scientists*, (Upper Saddle River, New Jersey: Merrill Prentice Hall, 2006), 31-32.
36 Neil Postman and Charles Weingartner, *Teaching as a Subversive Activity: A no-holds-barred assault on outdated teaching methods—with dramatic and practical proposals on how education can be made relevant to today's world*, (New York: Delacorte Press, 1969), 1.
37 Loewen, *Lies*, 313.
38 Constantin Stanislavski, *Creating a Role*, (New York: Routledge, 2003), 135.
39 Postman and Weingartner, *Teaching as a Subversive Activity*, 3.
40 John Dewey, *Experience and Education*, (New York: Touchstone, 1997), 61.
41 Gathercoal, *Judicious Discipline*, 17.
42 Dewey, *Experience and Education*, 28.
43 Dewey, *Democracy and Education*, 214.
44 Whitehead, *The Aims of Education*, 1.
45 L.S. Vygotsky, *Mind in Society: The Development of Higher Psychological Processes*, (Cambridge, Massachusetts: Harvard University Press, 1978), 94.
46 Whitehead, *The Aims of Education*, 30.
47 Ibid, 31.
48 Sharon Leon, "Interview with Exemplary Teachers: Nancy A. Hewitt," *The History Teacher* 38, no.3 (May 2005), 381.
49 Ibid.
50 Whitehead, *The Aims of Education*, 34.
51 Ibid.
52 Richard E. Mayer, "Should There Be a Three-Strikes Rule Against Pure Discovery Learning? The Case for Guided Methods of Instruction," *American Psychologist* 59, no.1 (January 2004), 14.

53 Ibid.
54 Ibid, 15.
55 Whitehead, *The Aims of Education*, 34.
56 Mayer, "Should There Be a Three-Strikes Rule," 15.
57 Whitehead, *The Aims of Education*, 36.
58 Maxwell Taylor Kennedy (Ed.), *Make Gentle the Life of this World: The Vision of Robert F. Kennedy*, (New York: Harcourt Brace and Company, 1998), 81.
59 Dewey, *Experience and Education*, 17.

Chapter Four
Avoiding the Bishop Trap

In 1950 the Vatican bestowed a patron saint on school teachers throughout the world. John-Baptist de La Salle (1651-1719) had been canonized in 1900 in part for his work founding schools for the poor and for his pioneering work in the training of teachers in France during the seventeenth and eighteenth centuries.[1] According to researcher David Hugh Farmer, La Salle's "two principal works reflect his life's main achievements: *The Conduct of Christian Schools* explains his widely praised educational methods and ideals, while his *Meditations for Sundays* reproduces his teaching on prayer."[2] One of the fundamental tenants of La Salle's educational philosophy was "the insistence on the silence of the pupils while the teaching took place."[3] Anyone who has read the rules posted on the walls of modern classrooms or who even remotely remembers their own school experience can clearly see how influential La Salle remains. His professed belief that students should remain quiet while the teacher passes down knowledge is alive and well in American schools. It is this belief, however, that often stands directly in the path of true education for our young.

John-Baptist La Salle may remain the patron saint of educators, but there is a more powerful example from Catholic tradition that we are better suited to keep in the forefront of our minds as we consider ways to fully implement constructivism in the teaching of history. This example is a cautionary tale for teachers. Bishop Fray Juan de Zumarraga is the man history teachers should think of when we walk into our classrooms. Although far from a household name, the bishop can tell us much about how and why we often fail our students. Bishop de Zumarraga served at Tenochitlan in central Mexico. Juan Diego, a poor, rural Aztec Indian brought to the bishop a request from the Virgin Mary for a temple to be built in her honor. Upon his first visit to the bishop, Diego was "kept...waiting for hours" by the bishop's servants.[4] According to tradition, the bishop did not take Diego's request too seriously, telling him at one point that he would consider the matter, and at another requesting a sign from the Holy Mother to prove the veracity of what Juan Diego was saying. Diego "was disappointed by the bishop's response and felt himself unworthy to persuade someone as important as a bishop."[5]

It is easy from a distance of nearly five hundred years to hold de Zumarraga in some contempt for his treatment of Juan Diego. His own clear disregard for the words of a peasant Indian may make us shudder and shake our heads. But we would do well to ask ourselves, as educators, how much of the bishop resides within us, especially within our classroom. Far too often the teaching certificates bestowed on young teachers comes with a willful pride and arrogance that we are now the state-supported font of knowledge for the children in our care. With this arrogance comes a lack of respect for the voice of our students, rendering to them the role of mute recipients of the frequently uninspired rhetoric of our lesson plan. Like Bishop de Zumarraga, we smile with forced patience as we gain control over our classes by silencing the children within them.

We must ask ourselves, however, if this is truly *education*? John Dewey certainly did not think so. Dewey wrote:

> Enforced quiet and acquiescence prevent pupils from disclosing their real natures. They enforce uniformity. They put seeming before being. They place a premium upon preserving the outward appearance of attention, decorum, and obedience. And everyone who is acquainted with schools in which this system prevailed well knows what thoughts, imaginations, desires, and sly activities ran their own unchecked course behind this façade.[6]

Surely enforcing uniformity is not the essence of a true education, particularly when we are approaching a topic such as history, which is so open to debate and opinion. Do we ask our students, as the bishop did, to provide us with a sign of the worth of their thoughts and natures before we extend to them the basic courtesy of treating them like human beings who have, as Dewey pointed out, "thoughts, imaginations [and] desires?" Every social studies teacher must face this question honestly if we are to insure that our pride and arrogance do not undermine our vocation.

There are three steps I propose we take to overcome this Bishop Trap. First, we must honor the importance of silence in our classroom—both that of our students and our own silence. Secondly, we must recall that the very nature of education lies in the give and take, the conversation, which must exist in our schools. Finally, we must reform our teacher training programs, so that young teachers have respectful behavior modeled for them before they are given their own classrooms.

In Defense of Silence

It is a sad comment on the state of our modern society that we feel such a desperate need to fill every waking hour of our day with some form of *noise*. We leave the television on though no one is watching. Our cars are tuned to radio stations although we are only casually listening. Our culture has an obsessive, almost preternatural fear of silence. It may be this fear which causes our nation to produce so few contemplatives. Introspection has become a lost art.

This fear also pervades our schools. Selma Wasserman has written a wonderful article entitled "Asking the Right Question: The Essence of Teaching." One of the issues she discusses is the prevalence of the "teacher answered question."[7] This occurs when the teacher asks a question and then, when an answer is not immediately forthcoming, answers it him or herself. There are many possible reasons for this reaction, although the most obvious is once again our fear of silence. Perhaps we have been trained to speak at any cost. After all, our culture teaches that those who are silent are believed to consent. This is a rather daunting assumption when one does not fully understand the context or the meaning of the conversation, as is the case for many students. Whatever the reason, the apparent need to fill the intellectual space of our classes with sound is destructive to the aims of education.

Parker Palmer has written that

> Psychologists say that a typical group can abide about fifteen seconds of silence before someone feels the need to break down the tension by speaking. It is our old friend fear at work, interpreting the silence as something gone wrong, certain that worthwhile things will not happen if we are not making noise.[8]

Our culture, then, affords the student fifteen seconds to weigh the pros and cons of the issues we place before them. Imagine, then, that as a social studies teacher your students have fifteen seconds to consider the impact of Dr. Martin Luther King. Jr.'s "I Have a Dream" speech on America. Or fifteen seconds to consider, formulate and become prepared to intelligently articulate their opinion on the impact of Watergate on modern political views and participation. The answers we receive, if we receive any at all, are likely to be superficial and disappointing.

Paradoxically, this fear of silence may cause the social studies teacher to ask his or her students well developed, thought-provoking questions, without giving the students ample time to *actually think* about them. The result is that students learn their answers must be quick or their voices will not be heard at all. The teacher and the teacher's opinions then become the focal point of the class. This makes our students little more than receptacles for our "knowledge." If the purpose of education is to impress students with all that we learned in college, then this is a satisfactory outcome. But if the purpose of education is to train students to think and then articulate their thoughts, then we have obviously failed.

Our discomfort with silence causes us to underestimate the abilities of our students. Palmer says:

> But suppose that my panic [at a prolonged silence] has misled me and my quick conclusion is mistaken. Suppose that my students are neither dumbfounded nor dismissive but digging deep; suppose that they are not ignorant or cynical but wise enough to know that this moment calls for thought; suppose that they are not wasting time but doing a more reflective form of learning. I

miss all such possibilities when I assume that their silence signifies a problem, reacting to it from my own need for control rather than their need to learn.[9]

Palmer is reflecting the need for a teacher not only to stand against our societal fear of silence, but also the need to combat cynicism. He acknowledges the possibility that his students might be wise and reflective. The cynical teacher assumes that the silence signifies ignorance or the wasting of time. Such cynicism is corrosive to the teacher's idealism and sets a very poor example for the students. Indeed, if we attribute only (or even predominately) negative motivations to our students' silence then we are showing them the ultimate form of disrespect.

If we truly wish to teach our students how to think then we must give them the room for thought. This means allowing time for our students to reflect and to be contemplative. A good history teacher will understand the need for silence; it is not something to be merely *tolerated*, but rather something that we should nurture with all our powers. Thomas Merton wrote that a "contemplative who tries to teach contemplation before he himself really knows what it is will prevent both himself and others from finding the true path to God's peace."[10] Merton is but one example of a contemplative, but his words on the subject are especially powerful. His statement places an added dimension of responsibility onto the teacher because we must practice what we preach. Not only will we build time for our students to practice contemplation in silence, but we will find time for ourselves as well.

Perhaps the most important aspect of honoring silence in our classes is that this stance shows a profound respect for the learner and their needs, opinions, and words. Ironically, allowing silence in our classroom will provide our students with the opportunity to have their voices heard. Our willingness to let young people contemplate a response, rather than demanding or expecting rote answers sends a clear message to our students: this teacher does not have all the answers, and we are all in this search together. In her autobiography, Zora Neale Hurston wrote about one of her favorite teachers. She wrote of him: "He radiates newness and nerve and says to your mind, 'There is something wonderful to behold just ahead. Let's go see what it is.' He is a pilgrim to the horizon."[11]

The description of her teacher as a pilgrim is lovely because it reminds us that we are on a journey with our students. Changing the role of history teachers from tour guides to fellow travelers can be begun by honoring the role of silence. Lakota medicine man Archie Fire Lame Deer puts the matter this way: "The humble upright-walker should not be all knowing. We are already too smart for our own good—very clever but seldom wise."[12]

The Role of Conversation

Of course education involves more than just silence. It should be our fervent hope that the opportunity for silence we afford our students will lead to a sharing of both intellectual and spiritual substance. Merton wrote that "Silence does not exist in our lives merely for its own sake. It is ordered to something else. Silence is the mother of speech."[13] Thus, the second aspect of teaching we must face if we are to value the voices of our students is the role of conversation within the classroom. By *conversation* I mean the quality of the give and take between teacher and student. Engaging students in a dialogue about the meaning and purpose of historical inquiry and the social studies curriculum allows them ownership of their educational process and, perhaps most importantly, their very heritage. James D. Kennedy, a North Carolina high school history and drama teacher for thirty years, described teaching as "a dialogue with humanity."[14] Such a view means that our students' voices must be heard and valued within the educational system. The catechism of the Catholic Church speaks to the value of conversation in this way:

> The background of all our speech is conversation: sitting companionably together and chatting unimportant things. This is one of the basic structures of our existence. It is a way in which we learn to know each other without hypocrisy or suspicion. Those who always take over a conversation and give others no chance are destroying something...To let someone talk himself out, to encourage him by our attention, can give great happiness.[15]

Although social studies teachers may quarrel with the "unimportant things" label mentioned above, the nature and role of conversation does not change even if we are discussing important things. Rather, the importance of conversation is enhanced in such a situation.

Respecting the role that conversation should play in the social studies classroom also serves another important function. That is, as the catechism phrases it so well, getting to know each other. To have effective conversation with our students we must get to know them as more than students, we must begin to know them and to view them as people. Harvard educator Vito Perrone asks simply, "How is it possible to teach students well without knowing them well?"[16] Getting to know and trying to understand our students extends to them a most basic courtesy and allows us to broaden the chances of our own success.

There are many ways to incorporate the conversational approach to education. The most obvious, perhaps, is by employing the tried but true Socratic Method of teaching. This method allows the student to find their own "truth" through probing and thoughtful questions prepared and asked by the teacher. In this method, the burden is removed from the teacher, who no longer must provide students with facts. Moreover, the Socratic Method cannot succeed without the voice of the student.

A method I have found very useful in my classroom is to set aside certain days for the purpose of having a discussion with my students about non-academic pursuits and concerns. Typically I will do this on the day immediately following a test. In that span between the old material and the new, we have a slight window for talking with our students about their lives. The students have (hopefully) studied hard for the test and gone through the stress of taking it. Rather than plunging ahead with the next chapter or unit, I will spend the next day asking them what *they* would like to talk about. It may be connected to the material we have just learned, but it need not necessarily be.

Such class periods are not wastes of time and should not be viewed by the teacher as a "day off." The first time a teacher tries it, he or she may be disappointed at the students' response. They are frequently concerned with "should we take notes on this" or other such school-system traps to which they have become accustomed. It may be hard for them to open up and trust us with their personal views and concerns. But if we stick with the approach, my experience has always been that it eventually yields invaluable benefits and results.

During these conversations I have learned that my sixth graders were already worrying about finding the money for a college education. I have learned that my tenth graders were terrified that some of their friends were becoming enslaved to drugs, alcohol, or eating disorders. Seventh grade girls were already weighing the risks of sexual activity with the burden of being labeled a "prude" and not being in the *in-crowd*. Knowing such things—knowing them by having experienced it through their voices rather than a scholarly report—made me a more compassionate and effective teacher.

Perrone wrote:

> When teachers know students well—their interests, learning patterns, general stance, the meaning of their gestures, their ways of approaching new materials and fresh ideas, and their outlook on the world—they can more productively engage them on a personal basis, ensuring a deeper entry into learning.[17]

If we allow ourselves to learn about our students on a personal basis, we make it vastly less likely that we should fall into the oldest of educational traps: viewing them as blank slates upon which we write. Such a view is not educational so much as it is authoritarian. The young men and women in our care do indeed have outside cares and concerns, hobbies and habits, with which we must deal with (and sometimes wrestle) every day. We cannot hope to deal with these successfully without first knowing what they are. Perrone argues that both intelligence and knowledge develop "from cooperative exchange."[18]

In a classroom in which cooperative exchange truly occurs, the teacher must be willing to humble him or herself. In the words of Gandhi, "The seeker after truth should be humbler than the dust."[19] Our students bring with them into the class all of their accumulated experience—these are not left at the school house door. By engaging our students and listening to them we let them know that we honor these experiences and that they are of value. The social studies textbooks may imply that racism ended in the United States with the signing of the Civil Rights Act of 1964, but students in the lower ninth ward of New Orleans know better than this. If the teacher is to have any credibility at all in that classroom, he or she will not toe the line of the textbook. The teacher, though older and perhaps wiser, still must care about the road on which our students are traveling.

Educators also have a responsibility to insure that our students have a say in the development and construction of their own knowledge, for they will surely one day navigate the treacherous terrain of their values and beliefs alone. The young must learn to synthesize their experiences with their hopes and dreams. If we honor their experiences, they are more likely to learn to trust their own instincts and act upon them. This is the very basis for the Greek word *praxis*, which means "action with reflection."[20]

Jay Martin has written of John Dewey's classroom approach that "teaching was an inquiry in which teachers and students formed a community of minds that 'saw together.' There was no dogmatism in this mode of instruction."[21] We may think back to the earlier discussion of the teacher as a fellow traveler. We may reasonably believe that we honor our vocation as teachers when we honor the experiences of students. As Merton eloquently wrote:

> Every moment and every event of every man's life on earth plants something in his soul. For just as the wind carries thousands of winged seeds, so each moment brings with it germs of spiritual vitality that come to rest imperceptibly in the minds and wills of men. Most of these unnumbered seeds perish and are lost, because men are not prepared to receive them.[22]

We effectively train the young to be ready to receive these seeds by respecting the fruit they bear; *we honor the experiences of youth.*

Our conversation, based as it must be upon the students' lives and experiences, also prepare students for active participation in a life dedicated to some form of social justice. The study of history should prepare students for their eventual role as leaders in a democratic society. If our students never experience responsibility in their young lives, they are less prepared to function responsibly in society as adults. In conversation with our students, we draw them into a world of issues and troubles in which they have a say; we empower them for later, when they are the leaders of our nation.

Such activity is both engaging and challenging, as education should be. Rather than merely relating stories of how others in the past have dealt with crises, we ask our students how they might deal with a crisis. Rather than blithely discussing a current controversy without resolution, we place the controversies in the laps of our students and allow them to wrestle with moral and political judgments. Active, rather than passive learning, may inspire generations of young people to answer for themselves Dorothy Day's question: "Where were the saints to try to change the social order, not just to minister to the slaves but to do away with slavery?"[23] Respectful conversation within our classes also answers Perrone's question: "Does it [education] mean ensuring that young people can live in the world as it is, or ensuring the skills, knowledge, and dispositions that will enable them to *change* the world, to construct on their own terms new possibilities?"[24] As long as we teach in a world in need of change, the answer to this question should remain self evident.

Asking our students to lend their voices to our conversation helps to instruct them in ways to speak out—to articulate—their own positions against injustice and inhumanity wherever they may encounter them. Empowering the young people we educate provides a role model for them, and encourages them to work for the empowerment and betterment of others. We hope that the challenges we place before them in the class may be carried out into their lives. Social activist Paul Rogat Loeb writes:

> Those of us who are relatively privileged are used to finding our interests and needs attended to. Contentedness, though, can induce insensitivity, even among people who are caring and generous. That's why we may consciously need to work to avoid becoming what Carol Bly calls 'lucky predators,' who by casually accepting the gifts bestowed by fortune, inadvertently circumscribe the lives and dampen the aspirations of countless others. No matter how well off we may be, we're spiritually impoverished whenever our society treats people with contempt, pillages the earth, or cannibalizes our common future.[25]

Any education which does not speak to the responsibilities of man to his fellow man is hardly worthy of the name.

Reforming Teacher Preparation

If it is our hope that social studies teachers may change their approach within the classroom in a way that truly values the voices of students, then we must first face the daunting challenge of changing the way these teachers are themselves prepared for their life's work. Ronny Russell is a minister in Locust, North Carolina, and a good friend of mine. He struggled for years with the challenge of bringing change to a church that was quite content in doing things the way they had always been done. Of this process he wrote that:

> Churches as systems have an awful propensity to suppress and even deny the existence of problems. Most pastors avoid conflict like the plague. We have strong tendencies toward suppression, denial, and avoidance of trouble and conflict. Many churches are not healthy systems in this way. They are dysfunctional, just like families.[26]

This diagnosis applies equally to our system of teacher preparation. Perhaps civil rights activist Will D. Campbell's observation is true when he asks, "What better way to neutralize an organization than to give it respectability?"[27]

The bestowing of respectability upon the preparation of teachers has caused too many to view and portray teaching as a science, with the possibility of replication across a diverse spectrum of communities and children. This view is not the same as viewing teaching as a *vocation*, with all the spiritual implications that word brings. Perrone has decried the tendency in modern teacher preparation programs to turn "...teachers into technicians, intermediaries for someone else's ideas and curriculum, with little concern for local circumstances."[28]

Those who train teachers have a responsibility to provide them with much more than merely the standard "methods and materials" approach. Pre-service social studies teachers need to be constantly reminded of the sacred obligation they take on once they decide to become a teacher. They are agreeing to become the gatekeepers of the American story and the story of civilization. They are saying that I may reasonably trust them to tell my story and my grandparents' story faithfully, accurately and passionately.

Pullias and Young have written that "A distinguished psychologist once said that there are three roles no sensible person should undertake: parent, statesman, or teacher. The relationships are so complex and often contradictory, the demands so inescapable, the stakes so high that a thoughtful person has a natural tendency to pull back from the responsibilities."[29] The men and women in teacher education courses, however, have decided *not* to pull back. They have decided to accept this challenge and to devote themselves, their abilities and their talents to the improvement of society through the education of our young. This is a clearly noble and idealistic decision. Those who are willing to step into the controversies involved in teaching history need to be prepared and trained by a system that constantly reminds them of these grand purposes. Sadly this does not appear to be happening.

Our current system for preparing educators fails to have future history teachers face the moral responsibilities and elements of their coming work. A 1998 study conducted by Jane Wells at Boston University found that "although teachers find that their job requires them to engage in moral education on a day-to-day basis, they received little or no preparation for this task in their pre-service teacher training programs."[30] The danger here is that teachers may well come away with the misguided impression that teaching history is simply about the transmission of knowledge. Such an impression is one of the reasons so many young people *positively hate* social studies—memorizing dates, names and capitols hardly captures or sparks the imagination. Examining and debating the moral issues of history—slavery, the bombing of Hiroshima and Nagasaki, and the Trail of Tears to name but a few—calls for a teacher who can navigate such dicey and potentially explosive issues. But we do not prepare future history teachers (or any others for that matter) for such pedagogical adventures.

This failure denies the fundamental foundation of education—purposeful, idealistic work with young people. Without this foundation, new teachers are likely to find their new job and its myriad roles bewildering. Helen McKenna, a high school science teacher of over twenty years, told author Ray Raphael the following about why she remained in the classroom despite her frustrations: "If I did quit teaching, I'm not really sure what else I'd get involved in. What are you going to do in society that's meaningful? And I do believe in meaningful work. Working with kids...is a very meaningful job in our society. One of the only ones."[31] Clearly her idealism allows her, even challenges her, to stay in the classroom and continue with her life's work. If we forget to nurture this idealism within teacher preparation programs, what will sustain the coming generations of educators?

Educator David T. Hansen unapologetically calls teaching, as I have, a "vocation." He defines the term as being "work that has social value and that provides enduring personal meaning."[32] Thus, those who endeavor to work with pre-service teachers need to make explicit the connections between their future careers and the social value and personal meanings of which Hansen writes. Educator Herbert Kohl argues that "Too many young people coming out of college believe that they do not know anything worth sharing or at least feel that they haven't learned anything in school worth it. Teacher training usually doesn't help since it concentrates on 'teaching skills' rather than the content of what might be learned."[33] This obvious divide between the understanding of teaching skills and methods and the knowledge of the grander purposes of education is tragic in that it diminishes both the responsibilities and the possibilities of a teacher. Those involved in teacher training should recall the words of Hansen, who wrote, "Teachers are not prophets, but neither are they interchangeable, *at least if one grants that teachers do more than mechanically transmit a mandated body of knowledge*" [emphasis added].[34]

One of my former pre-service students who now serves in the Peace Corps in Ghana, spoke about her frustration with the overly technical focus of her training. She said:

> I feel as if [students need to be] remind[ed]...why we are getting into teaching in the first place. We certainly are not in it for the money, or the respect, or any other selfish or material reasons. Generally, we are in it because we want to help, we want to make a difference, and we love kids. I think these ideas can get lost in the shuffle of the pedagogy and theories as we make our way through the education program.[35]

To answer this concern, I once piloted an experimental course in an education program that dealt exclusively with the aspects of social consciousness and idealism that are inherent in good teaching. One of the students in this class spoke eloquently about the need for such a course for pre-service teachers. He is quoted here at some length:

> I think classes like this...are as important, if not more important, than traditional education classes. We are not only teachers, but we are also citizens in a society. And, our profession as teachers also demands us to train our students, not only in respective disciplines, but to also train them to be good members of our society. I believe that a class like this can be very valuable to all teachers...
>
> It takes a good citizen to be a good teacher. I think that teachers should not only teach in a formal class setting, but also should teach by example and be a mirror of the kind of person they expect from the students. Social consciousness is a fundamental part of being a valuable person in a society.

A class in social consciousness is just as important to me as a teacher as any other pedagogy, lesson plan, and theory training that I am receiving. We need to have the ability to identify a social injustice, and to teach students how to identify them.[36]

Another student in the same class said, "As important as pedagogy and theories are for education majors, I think it is more important to talk realistically about what we can do to help change peoples' lives for the better. That is the reason why I got into teaching."[37] If we do not strive to remind future history teachers of the idealism and social value of their work, we run the very real risk of losing many of the best among them.

In addition to failing to provide pre-service teachers with a moral and social foundation for their work, those of us who work in the preparation of teachers may also be setting a poor example of valuing the voices of students. The mindset that the person at the front of the class is the font of all knowledge is certainly not confined to elementary and secondary settings. College professors who train pre-service social studies teachers are guilty of the same sort of arrogance. This arrogance should be deeply troubling because it often serves as the example these young men and women will emulate once they are in their own classrooms.

Many pre-service teachers—whether social studies or not—feel that their voices are not honored in their preparation programs. A recent study with seven pre-service teachers found that "The participants [in the study] discussed a nascent idealism they had felt when deciding to enter the teacher education program and become a teacher, but they felt that this idealism was hampered—not encouraged—by the program."[38] One of the participants talked about his desire to become a teacher this way: "I think...that you have to be an idealist to want to go into education...no matter what field you are or what age group...your kids are going to be coming from different backgrounds, different heritages, and it's important to understand that and to care about people. [Education] is pretty much about fellow citizens, fellow man, and that's important no matter what age group you're dealing with."[39] This young man felt, however, that holding on to this idealism was made more difficult by the proscriptive nature of his teacher education program. Palmer has written that the cynicism of college students "simply proves that when academic culture dismisses inner truth and honors only the external world, students as well as teachers lose heart."[40] Sadly, these students not only felt that their inner truth was dismissed, but also diminished.

Pre-service teachers may also feel that the "experts" responsible for their training fail to acknowledge or honor their experiences. A common complaint that I hear from future social studies teachers is that their professors seem to have all the answers, although many of them have not been in an elementary or secondary classroom for decades. In such situations, "pet" theories often fail to conform to the reality the students have recently lived. One of my pre-service teachers related a story in which, during a class discussion in the education program, he had shared an experience he had in his recent past at a high school.

The professor's response was unsettling and depressing, and it had angered this student greatly. He said:

> I had a teacher just basically say, 'Oh, well, it doesn't really happen, it's no big deal.' I said, 'I just gave you some real-world experience and you just told me that it doesn't happen!' That's the biggest thing that has turned me off about some of these college classes that I've had, so much of it's theory, which I understand you have to talk theory, but I think there needs to be more...the whole idealism and the real world stuff doesn't mesh.[41]

This student was clearly frustrated that his life experience had been so cavalierly dismissed by the professor. There is the possibility that his resentment will serve as a powerful reminder for him throughout his career and he will never ignore the experiences of his own students. But that is not a given, and the fact that such a poor example had been set for him in the program designed to train him for teaching must be a cause for great concern.

Henry Giroux wrote that "Teachers and other educational workers...often ignore questions concerning how they perceive their classrooms, how students make sense of what they are presented, and how knowledge is mediated between teachers (themselves) and students."[42] Ignoring such perceptions, however, is foolish and counterproductive. If pre-service teachers feel that their voices and experiences are not honored within their training programs, then they are likely to internalize this model as some form of "best practice." That is, they may well leave our universities thinking education is supposed to be a dictatorship. When this occurs, we are trapped in a damaging cycle that continually devalues the young.

When training those who will occupy the classrooms of the future, we should recall the words of Emerson, who wrote:

> I believe that our own experience instructs us that the secret of Education lies in respecting the pupil. It is not for you to choose what he shall know, what he shall do. It is chosen and foreordained, and he only holds the key to his own secret. By your tampering and thwarting and too much governing he may be hindered from his end and kept out of his own. Respect the [student]. Wait and see the new product of Nature. Nature loves analogies, but not repetitions. Respect the [student]. Be not too much his parent. Trespass not on his solitude.[43]

It is not our job to create clones—those who will teach to *our* strengths—but empowered artists who will know and teach to *their own* strengths. Former United States senator Gary Hart phrases it in this way: "Every man and woman must look within themselves for the noble spark, the human instinct, the core conviction that we are all in this together and will be judged by the nation we leave behind for future generations."[44] The professors who train pre-service social studies teachers may not be able to provide that noble spark, but it is indeed within our power to squelch it. It is against this that we must be ever vigilant.

Bishop Fray Juan de Zumarraga is forever etched in history for his arrogance towards Juan Diego. He will always be known as the man who, with no faith in his fellow man, demanded a sign. Although most teachers need not worry about such eternal infamy, we must stand guard against linking ourselves in the mind of even one student in a similar way. The good history teacher will be deeply humbled by his or her responsibility, and will evince this humility by listening, patiently and lovingly, to the voices of our students. We may take as our mantra the words of Saint Peter: "Should anyone ask you the reason for this hope of yours, be ever ready to reply, *but speak gently and respectfully.* Keep your conscience clear." Under our care young men and women will begin their search for meaning and understanding. Under our tutelage these same students will try and carve out a place for themselves in an ever changing and increasingly cynical world. Educators can help them in this search, but we cannot provide them with the destination.

Teachers of history must never forget that we, too, are students. If we have reached the point where we stop learning new things about the world around us and discovering new elements within our own soul, then we can no longer assist the young. We are not and never will be all-knowing. This is not a hindrance; it is the very basis for educating our students. We tell them: we shall be on this journey with you. Sometimes we will walk ahead of them. Other times, if we are humble enough, we will walk behind them, *and they will teach us.* This can only happen, however, if we are open to them and what they know, think, and feel. Honoring their voices allows educators to see the wondrous complexity of our jobs and our students. This must always be our primary goal.

---

1 David Hugh Farmer, *The Oxford Dictionary of Saints, Third Edition* (Oxford: Oxford University Press, 1992), 287-288
2 Ibid, 288.
3 Ibid.
4 *Our Lady of Guadalupe—Guadalupe, Mexico (1531) Patroness of the Americas.* Retrieved January 5, 2004 from http://www.catholic.org/about/guadalupe.html
5 Ibid.
6 John Dewey, *Experience and Education* (New York: Simon and Schuster, 1997), 62.
7 Selma Wasserman, "Asking the Right Question," Bloomington, IN: Phi Delta Kappa Educational Foundation.
8 Parker Palmer, *The Courage to Teach: Exploring the Inner Landscape of a Teacher's Life* (San Francisco: Jossey-Bass, 1991), 77.
9 Ibid, 82.
10 Thomas P. McDonnell (Ed.), *A Thomas Merton Reader* (New York: Image Books, 1989), 440.
11 Zora Neale Hurston, *Dust Tracks on a Road: An Autobiography* (New York: Harper-Perrenial, 1991), 107.

12 Archie Fire Lame Deer and Richard Erdoes, *Gift of Power: The Life and Teachings of a Lakota Medicine Man* (Sante Fe: NM: Bear and Company, 1992), 265.
13 McDonnell, *A Thomas Merton Reader*, 459.
14 James A. Bryant, Jr., *A Noble Discontent: The Experiences and Perceptions of Seven Pre-Service Teachers in an Experimental Course Designed to Examine the Relationship Between Social Consciousness and Education.* (Unpublished Dissertation, The University of North Dakota, 2003) 2.
15 *A New Catechism: Catholic Faith for Adults* (New York: The Seabury Press, 1973), 441.
16 Vito Perrone, *Lessons for New Teachers* (Boston: McGraw-Hill, 2000), 8.
17 Vito Perrone, *A Letter to Teachers: Reflections on schooling and the art of teaching* (San Francisco: Jossey-Bass, 1991), 27.
18 Perrone, *Lessons*, 36.
19 Mohandas K. Gandhi, *An Autobiography: The Story of my Experiments with Truth* (Mahadev Desai, Trans.), (Boston: Beacon Press, 1993), xxviii.
20 Jane Vella, *Learning to Listen Learning to Teach: The Power of Dialogue in Educating Adults* (San Franciso: Jossey-Bass, 1994), 11.
21 Jay Martin, *The Education of John Dewey: A Biography* (New York: Columbia University Press, 2002), 258.
22 McDonnell, *A Thomas Merton Reader*, 426.
23 Dorothy Day, *The Long Loneliness*, (New York: Harper and Row, 1952), 45.
24 Perrone, *Lessons*, 57.
25 Paul Rogat Loeb, *Soul of a Citizen: Living with Conviction in a Cynical Time* (New York: St. Martin's Griffin, 1999), 134.
26 Ronny Russell, *Can a Church Live Again? The Revitalization of a 21st Century Church* (Macon, GA: Smyth and Helwys, 2004), 70.
27 Will D. Campbell, *Brother to a Dragonfly,* (New York: Continuum, 2000), 242.
28 Perrone, *A Letter to Teachers,* 80.
29 Earl V. Pullias and J.D. Young, *A Teacher is Many Things,* (Bloomington, IN: Indiana University Press, 1968), 5.
30 Melinda Wells, *Teacher educators' conceptions of the responsibility of teachers as moral educators.* Dissertation abstract, Boston University, 1998.
31 Ray Raphael, *The Teacher's Voice: A Sense of Who We Are* (Portsmouth, NH: Heinemann), 71.
32 David T. Hansen, *The Call to Teach,* (New York: Teachers College Press, 1995), 9.
33 Herbert Kohl, *On Teaching* (New York: Schocken Books, 1976), 19.
34 Hansen, *The Call to Teach,* 11.
35 Bryant, *A Noble Discontent,* 95-96.
36 Ibid, 103.
37 Ibid, 104.
38 Ibid, 94.
39 Ibid, 95.
40 Palmer, *The Courage to Teach,* 19.
41 Bryant, *A Noble Discontent,* 99.
42 Henry A. Giroux, *Ideology, Culture and the Process of Schooling* (Philadelphia: Temple University Press, 1981), 37.
43 Ralph Waldo Emerson, *Selected Writings of Ralph Waldo Emerson* (New York: New American Library, 1965), 430.

44 Gary Hart, *The Patriot: An Exhortation to Liberate America from the Barbarians* (New York: The Free Press, 1996), 122.

Chapter Five
Beyond the Box

The sentence jumped off of the page and slapped me like a cold wind blowing in from the prairie. I had been sitting in my tacky, circa 1970 green chair in the living room of my home reveling in my geekiness by reading a fun book called *What Ifs? of American History*. The front jacket cover of the book proclaimed that inside "Eminent Historians" would dare to "Imagine What Might Have Been." The book had been a gift from my students at the University of New Orleans, and I had been devouring it and enjoying it as only some one with a passion for history could. Then I received the slap.

The chapter was entitled "Joe McCarthy's Secret Life" and was written by Ted Morgan. The sentence that gave me such pause came not in Morgan's fanciful essay, however, but in the introductory blurb that preceded it (therefore, I don't know whether to blame Mr. Morgan or the book's editor, Robert Cowley). Describing the excesses of the red-scare encouraging Wisconsin Senator Joseph R. McCarthy, the sentence read: "*Ever the Irishman*, he even went after America's chief ally, demanding that all British ships trading with Red China be sunk" [italics added].[1] I stared at the sentence and read it again several times. *Ever the Irishman*? What the hell did that mean? In context it seemed both obvious and appalling. The hardly subtle implication was that as a person of Irish descent, it was not-at-all surprising that McCarthy was hot-headed and seemed to be itching for any sort of fight. Ever the Irishman, you might say, was a clever little wink and nod to the fact that Irish folks aren't exactly stable or are prone to fits of irrational violence. Given that the essay itself dealt with McCarthy's chronic alcoholism and gambling habits, I became more and more offended at this off-the-cuff slur.

I wondered if the author of that line was even remotely aware of the struggles of Irish immigrants who came to America fleeing famine and loss. I wondered if the author of that line knew about the discrimination and violence that had met many Irish immigrants in their new American home. More than that, though, I wondered how such a ridiculous slur could have slipped past an editor at a reputable publishing house without someone throwing out, if you'll pardon the expression, a red flag. McCarthy may well have been a troglodyte, but impugning an entire section of the population hardly seemed justified, and to have occurred in a book written by "imminent historians" made it all the more troubling. It was enough to leave one scratching one's head about the state of diversity in the historical profession and, by extension, the social studies.

So what is the state of diversity issues in American history classrooms? Sadly, it is not much better than it was two decades ago. There have been all sorts of glossy, superficial changes in the textbooks and literally billions spent on diversity and sensitivity training for teachers of all curricula, but the net result has been more of the same, just packaged more cleverly with lots of bells and whistles. Whether called *diversity* or *multiculturalism*, the debate about moving social studies beyond just the stories of "great white men" has been a hot one. Unfortunately, the debate seems to have about as much middle ground as the fight over abstinence versus sex education. Caught between the Scylla and Charybdis of the politically correct and the traditional hagiography crowd, social studies teachers have found a compromise: teach about diversity in a way that is so utterly absurd and innocuous as to offend the smallest number of parents who actually know what is happening within their child's classroom. The result is a silly mess that should offend everyone.

To make the study of history relevant for all of our people, it is a moral imperative that we teach the history *of* all our people. This is not about Left or Right, liberal or conservative, it is simply about doing what is correct. It is unacceptable, for example, that a North Carolina history textbook could gloss over the tragedy of the Trail of Tears with a cute little box stuck in the corner of the page—but that is exactly what is happening right now in my home state. In the McDougal Littell textbook *North Carolina: A Proud State in our Nation*, the Cherokee people are mentioned a grand total of two times—this despite the fact that North Carolina has one of the largest American Indian populations east of the Mississippi River. One of those mentions is a disgraceful side-box (cleverly entitled "Historical Spotlight") that purportedly teaches about the Trail of Tears. There are too many problems with this boxed narrative for this chapter, but one that needs to be highlighted is the fact that *no mention* is made in the text that a single Cherokee Indian died on the Trail. The closest acknowledgment that is made is that the Cherokee "suffered greatly on their trek."[2] That's it; no mention that one out of four Cherokee died from this sorry moment in history. The textbook even dares to equate this tragedy to the "hardship" of "poor farming conditions...[and] lack of industry" faced by people of "European descent."[3] This tripe is brought to North Carolina's students from William S. Powell, a distinguished Professor Emeritus of History at the University of North Carolina at Chapel Hill. I don't know whether to be more offended as a person of Cherokee descent or as a UNC alum.

How did we arrive at such a point? In 1909 historian Ellwood P. Clubberly made the case that the function of social studies was one of "instilling into all a social and political consciousness that will lead to unity from diversity, and to united action for the preservation and betterment of our democratic institutions."[4] The key here is "unity from diversity"—a noble and necessary intention in American society. Unlike our counterparts in Europe and, indeed, across the globe, we are a nation without a truly common ancestry. Our people come from around the world to our shores as immigrants, searching for a better life. The most recent evidence indicates that even American Indians are one-time immigrants to this continent. However, Clubberly's intention loses something once it gets placed into practice. The emphasis on unity has served as a recipe not for embracing and understanding diversity, but for scuttling it.

It is possible to believe, as I do, that the only way to truly better our democracy and its institutions is through the understanding of the many divergent voices that make up America. The idea that we could club dissent by presenting only the "best" face of the nation has proven to be intellectually bankrupt. Our efforts at making social studies the hour of the day when students are instructed in their good fortune at having been placed here in this time and place has not managed to stop the riots in Watts, the "discovery" of Alcatraz, or the protests led by Cesar Chavez in the fields of California. With this is mind, many educators have begun to demand that the voices of all Americans be heard in our classrooms. The resulting arguments have become "fundamentally a battle over the idea of America."[5]

In this battle itself we see the folly of Clubberly's dream. Democracy is a messy business where unity is rare and the rhetoric can become heated. Not that you'd ever know that from your experience in social studies. Pearl Harbor comes and everyone agrees that we should now enter World War Two. The Declaration of Independence is signed and all colonists agree that war with Britain is now God's will. The attacks of September 11th, 2001, convince all Americans to rally behind the War on Terror. Unity becomes such a powerful theme in the way that we teach history that anyone who believes in or practices dissent is seen as little more than a frustrated old crank or, more insidiously, a traitor. Implicit in this pedagogy is an Orwellian message: difference is not a good thing—whether it is of opinion, class or race. Conform, we tell our students, and become good, cardboard cutout Americans. We saw this clearly in the ridiculous treatment of the Trail of Tears in the North Carolina textbook: let's quickly dispense with this small piece of ugliness and get back to our regularly scheduled programming: the heroic narrative of America.

Divisive issues such as the civil rights movement or the Indian wars of the nineteenth century as they are presented in social studies classrooms and texts serve only to portray American minorities as obstacles to our unity—obstacles that must be placated or steamrolled before the nation can get on with its important business, such as defeating communism or stretching America's boundaries to the West coast. James W. Loewen has studied the effect this portrayal has on minority students. "African Americans, Native Americans, and Latino students," he has found, "view history with a special dislike."[6] He has also found that these segments of our population do significantly worse in history than their white counterparts. The reason for this seems obvious—there is little within the history classroom to which they can relate. If their ancestors are shown as no more than standing in the way of the glorious Manifest Destiny of America, why would they want to spend any time studying this? American society offers enough to destroy minorities' self-esteem and sense of pride in their heritage on television and in popular culture each day, there is no need for a student to have these painful messages reinforced by his or her social studies teacher.

Issues of diversity are not, however, purely about fairness or even education. When it comes to the issues surrounding what knowledge is of most worth in a nation's historical narrative, the dominant force is *power*. It is by no means obvious that we should teach an inclusive history, and diversity and multiculturalism have ardent opponents. At times these opponents make cogent points, but just as often they appear to the world for what most of them are: members of a dominant cultural and political elite terrified of losing their centuries-old grip on the judgment of history. Tammy Bruce has made a career out of attacking anything that seems "Leftist," and her vitriol over multiculturalism is almost pathological. The sixth chapter of her book *The New Thought Police* is entitled "Multiculturalism: Thought Police in Costume."[7] "Multiculturalism," Bruce informs her reader, "...amounts to the Balkanization of this country into blacks, Asians, Native Americans, Hispanics, and so on."[8] Ms. Bruce doesn't deny that there *is* great diversity in America; she apparently just doesn't want us to talk about it. In order to dismantle the argument for diversity or multiculturalism, Bruce sets up a series of straw men and knocks them over with relative ease—although with little integrity.

Her first straw man comes from the tragic beating death of Kyuang-Ja Chung in Century City, California. Mrs. Chung was savagely beaten by her husband, Jae Whoa Chung, and another man (Sung Soo Choi, a Korean Pentecostal Christian minister, who Bruce refers to only as an "accomplice") in what they believed was a demon-cleansing ritual, or exorcism. Mrs. Chung's injuries were so brutal that the medical examiner said they resembled the injuries one would sustain if struck by a car.[9] Ms. Bruce's understandable indignation comes from the fact that the two men were tried and found guilty only of involuntary manslaughter. Jae Whoa Chung was sentenced to the maximum two years and Sung Soo Choi to four years in state prison—also the maximum allowed under the law—for involuntary manslaughter.[10] Bruce tells her readers that the judge in the case, Malibu Superior Court's James Albracht, was swayed by what she calls a "cultural defense."[11]

The case is a bit more complicated than Ms. Bruce would have one believe, however. Culture certainly played a role in Judge Albracht's decision, but he himself said at the time of the sentencing that he was moved more by the fact that the defendants had not acted maliciously. He also admitted finding the case difficult because "these are not subjects with which we routinely deal in the criminal justice system."[12] Albracht said that "These men, misguided as they were, did not act in conscious disregard for human life, but with a real, possibly tunnel vision, regard for it."[13] The Deputy District Attorney in the case, Hank

Goldberg, argued that the men should have known that their blows would cause Mrs. Chung to die and that the defendants waited too long to call for help—but not that they had intentionally set out to murder the victim.

Albracht also said, "As all sides know, I heard this case from start to finish. I'm struck by the tragedy to all people whose lives were touched by this case, but I can't escape that a good, honest woman and mother of two children...is dead."[14] This statement came after he had heard the defense attorneys argue for probation and listened to Mrs. Chung's children tearfully ask for leniency for their father. Again, there is a great deal of complexity here which Ms. Bruce denies her reader the opportunity to consider.

But the point here is not even to defend the decision of one California judge in a tragic and bizarre case. Ms. Bruce blames multiculturalism for the fact that Mr. Chung and his minister were not fried in San Quentin's electric chair. Someone should remind her of that old law school axiom: *hard cases make bad law*. While the Chung case is fascinating, Bruce offers not a shred of evidence to support her contention that this poor woman died as a result of teaching diversity in our schools or arguing for respect for diversity in our country. She tries to use sensationalism to camouflage the fact that her premise is factually specious at best, intellectually dishonest at worst. Christianity, after all, is hardly a minority in the United States, and exorcisms are sanctioned and performed by the Vatican and most Protestant denominations—also not minority groups in America. Demons are fought and tossed out by Anglo-Americans as well as Korean Pentecostals. Bruce writes that "We are becoming so hypnotized by the mantra of 'tolerance,'...that we are losing sight of our moral compass and are mindlessly embracing anything that's 'different.'"[15] Unless Christianity has recently become a religious order existing on the fringes of American society, drawing this conclusion from the Chung case alone is preposterous.

Bruce doesn't limit her attack to Judge Albracht, though. She also takes on the politically-charged issue of bilingual education, again using the most egregious and outlandish example—in this case the moronic Ebonics movement—to paint all supporters of multiculturalism or diversity as radicals out to destroy the very fabric of this nation. She has particular disgust for those who, like Jose Gonzalez of Columbia University Teachers College, argue that Spanish has now become a second national language in the United States. Ms. Bruce writes:

> For over three hundred years, people have left everything behind in their native lands, sometimes even risking their lives, in order to come to America and explore the dream and the reality of freedom. They did not come here to live in a little isolated version of their homeland.[16]

Immigrants have left *everything* behind? Given that Ms. Bruce's work is not written in Cherokee, I take particular umbrage with that idea.

That's the point here, though, isn't it? Bruce has sarcastic asides and sardonic quips for all sorts of different groups (it's a kind of diversity, I suppose), from Mexican workers to black school children to American Indians. But noticeably absent from her tirades against the Balkanization of America is any mention whatsoever of white separatists or white supremacists. She is abundantly clear in her preference: America means Western, European, and white. "The culture exists *as American*," she writes, "only because of assimilation."[17] Later in the same chapter she writes, "The demonization of certain cultures and complaints that people of those cultures are controlling society can be, as most notably in Nazi Germany, the opening salvos of tragic and violent attacks."[18] So there you have it—Hitler's love of diversity and insistence on a multicultural and pluralistic society led to the Holocaust. It has become *de rigueur* these days to shield a vacuous argument by having the image of the Nazis goose-step out onto the stage. It doesn't quite have the desired effect here, though. Although she provides token nods to the need for tolerance in a democratic society, Bruce's polemic comes across as the writings of someone embittered by the simple fact that minorities in America are now demanding that their story be told respectfully and accurately.

Bruce's anti-multiculturalist approach is not nearly as depressing as the more subtle but equally disturbing words of historian Walter A. McDougall of the University of Pennsylvania and the Foreign Policy Research Institute. McDougall wrote an eloquent piece for the National Council of History Education's newsletter, *History Matters!*, entitled "The Three Reasons We Must Teach History." The piece is moving and inspirational throughout most of the text, and it is not until the end that one begins to get the feeling that McDougall is about to drop a rhetorical bomb on the reader. This feeling grows when he quotes "eminent world historian" William H. McNeill's advice for the choices that need be made in preparing a history curriculum: "...just as some facts are more important to know than others, so have certain cultures displayed skills superior to those of others in every time and place in history...There is no use asserting that your culture is just as good as his. It palpably isn't...Superiority and inferiority, real and perceived, are the substance of human intercourse and the major stimulus to social change throughout history."[19] McDougall continues:

> McNeill's principle is no less applicable to U.S. history. An honest history must hear and pass on the laments of those displaced (including many white males) in the course of our nation's growth. But the main story line must remain that of the Euro-American dominant culture, its ideals and aspirations, creativity and service to itself and others in peacetime and war: the good as well as the bad and ugly.[20]

We are right back to the idea of the non-white as nothing more than an obstacle to the great American tale of grandeur and mystique.

In Professor McDougall's curriculum the history teacher's duty is to make room for the "lament" of the diverse—racially, culturally or economically. It is a curriculum where poor whites, American Indians, African Americans and others are the consummate whiners and, of course, always losers. The question that begs to be asked here is, however, what if some or all of these groups played parts in the American story that they want celebrated? Suppose that American Indians not only wish for the Trail of Tears, Wounded Knee and Sand Creek to be in the texts, but also the story of Ira Hayes helping to hoist Old Glory on Iwo Jima? Or perhaps they would like the story of the Navajo code talkers in World War Two included? Or maybe they would like to see the unbelievable athleticism of Jim Thorpe acknowledged? Perhaps African Americans wish to have W.E.B. DuBois taught as well as slavery. Could it be that African Americans contributed something to American culture other than constantly agitating for more group rights? McDougall's vision for the role of "those displaced" in the social studies curriculum is sad and unacceptable. It would simply displace non-whites and poor whites all over again. We can do better.

At the heart of these conservative attacks on diversity in history is what is, in fact, at the heart of all conservatism—fear. There is a fear of change, a fear of the dispersal of power, at work in the writing of Bruce, McDougall and their ilk. We must move the debate about the form and substance of a diverse historical perspective away from the tired and foolish notion that to teach from a multicultural perspective means to denigrate the accomplishments and contributions of white Americans and white America. This is an absurd excuse for not teaching a multicultural and diverse perspective when and where appropriate. An integrated, multicultural approach is not something parents or educators need to fear. There were, after all, whites fighting in the Civil War for the eradication of slavery. White men such as Will Campbell (himself a Southern Baptist from Mississippi) marched alongside Dr. King. And it was a white minister, Samuel Worchester, who went to prison in Georgia fighting for the rights of the Cherokee Nation against Andrew Jackson. So a multicultural perspective and curriculum is not anti-white; it is just not exclusively white. This argument is a shallow attempt to derail efforts at getting the accurate stories of minorities and oppressed groups into the classroom. Fear is a tremendous motivator.

The Immigration Act of 1965 brought a wave of immigrants during the 1970s that has continued to this day. Combine this new constituency with a heightened sense of racial consciousness and identification that was the result of the civil rights movement of the 1960s and 1970s, and it becomes clear that the stories of dead, rich white men that made up the social studies curriculum for so long is no longer sufficient because it no longer speaks to our students' needs.[21] Current philosophical trends in education trumpet the need for making the material relevant to the lives of our students. This will never happen in the social studies unless our history is told in terms that are significantly more inclusive. Teachers in America are already predominately white (91.8%, as compared with 66.1% of the student population)—our curriculum should not be so monolithic.[22] By moving our approach to social studies away from a strictly European point of view and more towards the rich heritage of America, we will soon find ourselves with a "curriculum of empowerment."[23]

America is not a homogenous society. For students to be presented with a homogenous history is, therefore, misleading and a grave distortion. Again, this is not an argument for the removal of Thomas Jefferson from the textbook—it is an argument for the inclusion of Sally Hemmings. There is a growing consensus among social studies educators that "it is imperative that young people recognize cultural pluralism as important to our understanding [the] past and preparing for the future since the majority of the world's population are non-European and people of color."[24] Fostering a sense of false inferiority among minority students for the sake of "unity" must no longer be acceptable in our nation's classrooms. As each ethnic group has contributed to the cultural and societal landscape of America, so must their contributions in the halls of power and on the field of battle be told. This is our duty.

The effort to teach a diverse, multicultural view of history is not only harmed by conservatives, however. If the road to hell is indeed paved with good intentions, then it often seems that liberals have a monopoly on asphalt. While a diverse social studies curriculum need not (and should not) be anti-white, there is little doubt that many leftists have urged just such a course. The purpose of social studies is certainly not to create thoughtless little robotic patriots, but neither is it to create guilt-ridden, neurotic cynics. Too often liberal pedagogy seems designed to assign blame and to create a sense of corporate guilt. Young people—to their eternal credit—categorically reject such garbage. A 16-year-old living in Boone, North Carolina, in 2006 is not willing to accept blame for the cancer of slavery, and well he should not. Original Sin is a fascinating theological concept; it has no relevance or place in a classroom devoted to history (unless, of course, it is a classroom examining the history of religion).

Original sin and corporate guilt are exactly what Gary R. Howard is about in his book *We Can't Teach What We Don't Know: White Teachers, Multiracial Schools*. In Howard's eyes, whiteness is a kind of curse on humanity that must be overcome. Howard's biographical blurb at the end of his book says that he "has been working with colleagues throughout the United States and many other parts of the world to bring a healing vision to schools, universities, and other organizations." His "healing vision" calls for, first and foremost, the acceptance by all white people of their historical guilt in the oppression of peoples across the globe. This is an interesting thesis given the definition of prejudice as written by multicultural education expert Christine I. Bennett. Bennett defines prejudice as "an attitude based on preconceived judgments or beliefs (usually negative) that develops from unsubstantiated or faulty information."[25]

With that definition in mind, it becomes clear that Howard holds significant prejudice against white people (despite that fact that he is white, a fact he seems utterly apologetic about throughout his book). "Honesty," he writes, "begins for Whites when we learn to question our own assumptions and acknowledge the limitations of our culturally conditioned perceptions of truth."[26] The tragedy of this sentence is that it would be a grand definition of *all* education if Howard did not suffer from such incredible myopia. Could not all races and classes and nationalities benefit from questioning assumptions and acknowledging the limitations of our perceptions of truth? Why is this statement confined to whites?

Because Howard's narrative is a classic case of over-correction: as a reaction to the false and racist notion that American and world history is a tale of only white genius and success, Howard and others jerk the pendulum in the extreme, casting "White" as the ultimate and sole villain in all of recorded history.

Howard finds the roots of White evil in the Christian faith. He sees the notion of a "chosen people" as the beginnings of white corruption.[27] While having clear contempt for the Catholic faith, Howard gives people of Jewish heritage something of a pass on this score. It is an interesting and telling decision. In the Old Testament, the "chosen people," after all, is a reference to the *Jewish* people. But because *Jew* isn't an equivalent of *white*, Howard conveniently doesn't pass his harsh judgment onto them. He also has nothing to say about the Muslim conception and teaching that all non-Muslims are infidels. He praises American Indian spirituality, however, as a model for the world. Howard apparently doesn't know that at least one indigenous society—the Cherokee—shared some of these traits he ascribes to white Christians. The word *Cherokee*, for instance, is a bastardization of the word *Tsalagi*, which is what this American Indian nation actually called itself. Tsalagi means "the principle people." The Cherokee believed that their society was the center of the entire universe and that all life and creation emanated out from them. While I could be wrong, this sounds like the concept of a "chosen people" to me.

Howard writes that he wants Whites to feel "enlightened" instead of "blamed."[28] Yet his assumptions about Whites are really based upon a homogenous cultural, political and economic elite that does not really exist. I have seen heartbreaking poverty in the inner cities of New Orleans and Baltimore, and more often than not it did, indeed, have a black face. But I have also seen gut-wrenching poverty in the mountains of Appalachia, and it has a white face. To be sure there is dominance and oppression in America and throughout the world, but it is based on economic realities, not pigment. Howard and others do a terrible disservice to the cause of equality and freedom when they peddle this racial dominance theory. History is infinitely more complicated than the dominance of one "race" over the globe. Many scholars have even rejected the very notion that there is anything such as "White." Does Howard mean the Irish, the English, Jewish, Italian? And is it not intellectually problematic to lump such a large and disparate group of ethnicities into one category?

When it comes to white people in general and white educators and students specifically, Howard is operating from what has been described as a deficit model. Typically this model is applied to school children from an impoverished socioeconomic background. Those children are viewed as coming from "an environment that retards children's overall development and leads to their disadvantage in school."[29] Bennett argues that the deficit model "stands in opposition to the philosophy of multicultural education," but it is the foundation of Howard's thesis.[30] His sweeping generalizations about "White people" would be decried if they were made about any other racial "group," as well they should be. His premise: that Whites must overcome their Whiteness before they can be humane and effective educators is as offensive as it is trite.

Arthur M. Schlesinger, Jr. reminds us that, "History remains a weapon," but he also reminds us that one need not be white to wield this weapon.[31] Schlesinger is concerned with the dividing up of history into racial components and, specifically, the move in New York City at the time of his essay toward an Afro-centric program of historical study. Rather than seeing race as the defining issue, he writes "The issue is the teaching of *bad* history under whatever ethnic banner."[32] He decries the move by liberals toward a blame-and-guilt curriculum and fears the most significant "casualty is the old idea that whatever our ethnic base, we are all Americans together."[33] Schlesinger is not arguing to sweep the histories of American ethnic minorities under the proverbial rug, but he sees real danger in the movement to make American history the province of any one group—whether white or otherwise. He writes:

> The use of history as therapy means the corruption of history as history. All major races, cultures, nations have committed crimes, atrocities, horrors at one time or another. Every civilization has skeletons in its closet. Honest history calls for the unexpurgated record. How much would a full account of African despotism, massacre, and slavery increase the self-esteem of black students? Yet what kind of history do you have if you leave out all the bad things?[34]

The desire by many on the Left to cast Whites as villains and to cast all others as victims leads inexorably towards a slanted and inaccurate history—the very thing the Left began fighting against.

Moreover, to portray any race as passive victims rather than active participants in the great scheme of history is to treat that race like wounded children. Such a paternalistic outcome cannot be the aim of historical study if we are to achieve a true curriculum of empowerment or even to address the wrongs of one group against another. The "Great White Father (or Mother)" notion of history is not something to which any of us should aspire, for it denies both responsibility and credibility to the story of a nation or a people.

Historian Diane Ravitch sums up the failure of many liberals well. She writes that, "What was once a fairly sensible notion of fairness—don't always show women as homemakers—has turned into a presumption that [women] should never be shown in that role."[35] Ravitch's point is a powerful one: in an effort to bring about equity in the gender roles presented in school books and tests, we have allowed women who choose to stay home for whatever reason to be chased out of the dialogue and essentially labeled as anachronistic, archaic, or just plain backwards. Call it reverse sexism, if you please, but it is an outcome that should be found equally as offensive as portraying *all* women as stay-at-home moms. Unfortunately, it isn't viewed that way at all; it is called progress.

Ms. Ravitch is wonderfully unambiguous about calling this progress what it is: censorship. At one point she writes of both left and right pressure groups:

"...book censorship far exceeds reasonableness; usually, censors seek not just freedom from someone else's views, but the power to impose their views on others."[36] The left's reaction to stereotyping in textbooks has been to cleanse texts of anything that might remotely smack of a stereotype. The result is that much of what passes for social studies has a sad, through-the-looking-glass quality to it. Faithfully teaching from such texts makes the curriculum and the teacher seem painfully out of touch or criminally aloof. Neither is likely to inspire any student to look forward to social studies.

One example that Ravitch cites of this other-worldly quality of the texts that result from pressure from the political left comes from a twelfth grade history textbook. She writes:

> A headline in a twelfth-grade history textbook read: 'Death Stalks a Continent: In the dry timber of African societies, AIDS was a spark. The conflagration it set off continues to kill millions.' The editor deleted it with the comment: 'Too full of inappropriate issues, too negative, we don't want to portray Africa as AIDS-ridden.'[37]

Of course any even partially informed citizen is aware of the horrible epidemic of AIDS that threatens African cultures and the peoples of Africa. While such knowledge is certainly depressing, to turn away from it, or to purposefully shield American students from it (twelfth graders, no less), is cowardly and inexcusable. As Ravitch points out, "With everything that might offend anyone removed, the textbooks lacked the capacity to inspire, sadden, or intrigue their readers."[38]

As good as her writing is, perhaps the most frightening and frustrating part of Ravitch's book comes in the appendices. Here she provides lists of images and words that have been banned by certain textbook publishers and testing agencies such as the Educational Testing Service (ETS). The list of images for American Indians is instructive due to the historical validity and importance of those that have been banned. MacMillan McGraw Hill (MMH), one of the major history textbook publishers, has banned any images depicting American Indians performing a "rain dance."[39] The implication is that such a portrayal would be historically inaccurate. This is not a valid, assumption, however. Historian James Axtell of the College of William and Mary provides an account from Robert Beverly's 1705 work on Indian religion in Virginia in which an overseer contracts with a local Indian for rain on his master's drought-stricken crops. The overseer promised the American Indian rum if he could provide the rain. He did not expect the Indian to make good on this deal, however, "not seeing at that time the least appearance of Rain, nor so much as a cloud in the sky."[40] Beverly recorded the final outcome as follows:

> Upon this the Indian went immediately a Pauwawing, as they call it; and in about half an hour, there came up a black Cloud into the Sky, that shower'd

down Rain enough upon this Gentlemans Corn and Tobacco, but none at all upon any of the Neighbors, except a few drops of the Skirt of the Shower.[41]

Under the guidelines imposed by MacMillan McGraw Hill, this fascinating primary document would be banned from view for American students of all races—and all in the name of diversity.

Holt Reinhart and Winston (HRW) have banned images of American Indians "in low-paying jobs, drunk, unemployed, or on welfare," and "living in shacks on reservations, with outdoor water tanks and bleak landscapes."[42] The ETS has banned images of American Indians "living in rural settings on reservations."[43] Both MMH and HRW have banned images depicting American Indians with "long hair, braids, [and] headbands."[44]

I am certainly not advocating portraying American Indians *only* in the ways described above. It is hard to fathom, however, how a history teacher could possibly do justice to American Indian history without some or even all of those images that have been banned. Examining the list of banned words and images, one is struck by the number of portrayals of American Indian life *by* American Indians that would not be allowed. The marvelous films *Skins* or *Smoke Signals* would not meet the stated criterion. Books by American Indian authors Leslie Marmon Silko, Louise Erdrich, Sherman Alexie, and John (Fire) Lame Deer would not be acceptable. In fact my own novel, *Curley*, based on the *real life* experiences of my grandfather Russell Norris would never meet these demands. *Curley* would be banned from schools because my grandfather was born on a rural reservation in North Carolina (Taboo One), struggled with alcoholism (Taboo Two), and spent his entire life working blue collar jobs and struggling financially (Taboo Three). In the effort to abolish stereotypes, liberals have failed to acknowledge the uncomfortable fact that most stereotypes have some basis in reality. Ravitch's observation about the portrayal of women applies equally well to American Indians and to many other minority groups.

Good education, like good policy, is rarely found at the extremes. While diversity and multicultural perspectives are essential to the reformation of the way in which we teach history, there must be an interjection of common sense to the debate. Good multicultural education exists somewhere between the cacophony of shrill voices from the right and left. We must expand our notions of what diversity means in history, and we must make it our cause to tell the full, unvarnished truth about America. This includes the contributions—not just the laments—of America's minority groups. This should not be done at the expense of any one group, whether it be White people or otherwise. We should not make room for Malcolm X by expunging George Washington; *we must make room for both*. To do so means more history in the curriculum from kindergarten through the high school years.

When I taught tenth grade American history, I was terrified at the magnitude of my assignment: teach from the pre-Columbian era to Clinton—in one academic year. The result is that all groups—not just minorities—get desperately short-changed. To spend only three days discussing the American Civil

War is downright criminal. Four days on the American Revolution is immoral, and yet this was the timeline I had—and I still barely got my students past FDR—and all this with an end-of-course test hanging over my head. Under such circumstances there is no way to do justice to the nuances and diversity of American history. One year spent on world history, it should go without saying, is a complete joke. Therefore, if multicultural history is to become a reality, then we must place a higher priority on the teaching of history and expand the curricular time frame so that we can teach not just more history, but a better, fuller history.

In addition to the time needed to bring the many textures and stories of history alive, we must move beyond the notion that diversity means the assignment of guilt and blame. Slavery existed among the indigenous peoples of the Americas as well as among African kingdoms—to portray it as a scourge of Europe only is false. To do so to appease the political left does not make it any less wrong. America has not always been the shining city on a hill of popular mythology, and to pretend otherwise to score points with the political right will never erase that fact. Ravitch wonders if history test scores are so dreadfully low because "with...teenagers' usual ability to spot a scam, they know that much of what is taught to them is phony and isn't worth remembering."[45]

The goal of an inclusive, multicultural social studies should be *E Pluribus Unum*. Our national motto, though clichéd by politicians over the years, is precisely the point of expanding the narrative of history to include all groups and their contributions. "Out of the many, One" is a beautiful vision. It has not always been true in this or any country, but it is the ideal for which we strive. As Ravitch writes, "The great drama of American history...was the conflict between the nation's ideals and its practices."[46] We fool no one with simplistic tales of purely good or purely evil history and historical figures. Man is a complicated, fascinating and intriguing animal. Humanity is both noble and decadent, often within moments of each other, and students know this even from the earliest age. America is a nation made up of many, and despite right wing protestations to the contrary, being proud of this fact does not weaken us. Yet, to truly achieve the American ideal, we come together as much as possible and we function as a collective and remarkable One. Despite what many on the left might claim, this does not weaken us, either.

As Saint Paul wrote in his first letter to the people in Corinth, "Our bodies have many parts, but the many parts make up only one body...Some of us are Jews, some are Gentiles, some are slave and some are free. But the Holy Spirit has fitted us all together into one body." History, fate, destiny, or luck has fitted the many peoples who make up America together, and this is a fact we should celebrate, study, and acknowledge. We have nothing to fear from diversity except that young generations will develop an appreciation for the veritable miracle that is America. There are far less appealing outcomes.

---

1 Ted Morgan, "Joe McCarthy's Secret Life," in *What Ifs? of American History: Eminent Historians Imagine What Might Have Been,* ed. Robert Cowley (New York: G.P. Putnam's Sons, 2003), 205.
2 William S. Powell, *North Carolina: A Proud State in our Nation* (Evanston, IL: McDougal Littell, 2003), 195.
3 Ibid.
4 Daniel Tanner and Laurel Tanner, *Curriculum and Development: Theory into Practice* (Upper Saddle River, New Jersey: Merrill, 1995), 85.
5 Ibid.
6 James W. Loewen, *Lies My Teacher Told Me: Everything Your American History Textbook got Wrong* (New York: Touchstone Books, 1995), 12.
7 Tammy Bruce, *The New Thought Police: Inside the Left's Assault on Free Speech and Free Minds* (New York: Random House, 2001), 145.
8 Ibid, 146.
9 Ibid, 149.
10 Amy Koval, "Exorcism," from City News Service, April 24, 1997. Retrieved from Lexis-Nexis December 21, 2005.
11 Bruce, *The New Thought Police,* 149.
12 Koval, "Exorcism," from City News Service, April 16, 1997. Retrieved from Lexis-Nexis December 21, 2005.
13 Amy Koval, "Exorcism," from City News Service, April 16, 1997. Retrieved from Lexis-Nexis December 21, 2005.
14 Koval, "Exorcism," from City News Service, April 24, 1997. Retrieved from Lexis-Nexis December 21, 2005.
15 Bruce, *The New Thought Police,* 152.
16 Ibid, 158-59.
17 Ibid, 148.
18 Ibid, 166.
19 Walter A. McDougall, "The Three Reasons We Must Teach History," *History Matters!* 17 No.2 (October 2004), 7.
20 Ibid.
21 Joel Spring, *American Education* (Boston: McGraw-Hill Higher Education, 2000), 148.
22 Ibid, 154.
23 Ibid, 159.
24 Margaret A. Laughlin and H. Michael Hartoonian, *Challenges of Social Studies Instruction in Middle and High Schools* (New York: Harcourt Brace College Publishers, 1995), 265.
25 Christine I. Bennett, *Comprehensive Multicultural Education: Theory and Practice* (Boston: Allyn and Bacon, 2003), 77.
26 Gary R. Howard, *We Can't Teach What We Don't Know: White Teachers, Multiracial Schools* (New York: Teachers College Press, 1999), 69.
27 Ibid, 55.
28 Ibid, 27.
29 Bennett, *Comprehensive Multicultural Education,* 241.
30 Ibid, 243.

31 Arthur M. Schlesinger, Jr., "The Disuniting of America," in Taking Sides: Clashing Views on Controversial Educational Issues, Eleventh Edition, Ed. James Wm. Noll (Guilford, CT: Dushkin/McGraw Hill, 2001), 271.
32 Ibid, 275.
33 Ibid, 278.
34 Ibid, 277.
35 Diane Ravitch, *The Language Police: How Pressure Groups Restrict What Students Learn* (New York: Alfred A. Knopf, 2003), 26.
36 Ibid, 77.
37 Ibid, 110.
38 Ibid, 111.
39 Ibid, 189.
40 James Axtell, *The Indian Peoples of Eastern America: A Documentary History of the Sexes* (Oxford: Oxford University Press, 1981), 198.
41 Ibid, 198.
42 Ravitch, *The Language Police,* 189.
43 Ibid.
44 Ibid.
45 Ibid, 156.
46 Ibid, 151.

Chapter Six
It's the Telephone Poles, Stupid

Goethe tells us that, "He only earns his freedom and existence who daily conquers them anew." Maybe this should be the mantra of all social studies teachers, because it is a sentiment that seems to stand in direct contrast to the lazy, modern notion that our freedoms are guaranteed by the government and vigilance is no longer necessary. Such laissez faire attitudes about democracy are perhaps the best antidote *for* democracy. We must find a way to communicate to the young people in our care that they do not have the luxury of taking for granted what has been bought at so high a price. Robert F. Kennedy, in a planned biography of his father Joseph Kennedy, wrote, "You knew that what is given or granted can be taken away, that what is begged can be refused; but that what is earned is kept, that what is self-made is inalienable, that what you do for yourselves and for your children can never be taken away."[1] Combining the sentiments of Goethe and Kennedy, it is our charge to show our students in social studies classes across America that freedom is tenuous and that we must daily conquer it anew.

Preceding generations understood this. Not yet spoiled by a social studies curriculum that engrained in their impressionable minds the belief that America was guaranteed victory and morality by Destiny, the early generations of Americans were well aware that ideals of freedom, equality and justice were difficult to attain and keep. As historian Joseph J. Ellis has written, "Securing a revolution has proven to be a much more daunting assignment than winning one."[2] That is the work of social studies teachers and should be the purpose of the social studies curriculum: to secure the American Revolution. Despite rumors (and textbook notions) to the contrary, the American Revolution did not end at Yorktown, nor did it end with the signing of the Treaty of Paris. It did not even end in 1789 as the Founders came back together to provide their nation with a written constitution. The American Revolution and its ideals and dreams are a work in progress. These ideals are constantly refined and, hopefully, as a people we continue to progress towards a more perfect rendering of them. But we may never take them or such progress for granted.

When Benjamin Franklin emerged from the oppressive heat of Independence Hall in Philadelphia, a woman on the street came up to him and asked what kind of government the constitutional convention had given the new nation. He is reported to have replied, "A republic, madam, *if you can keep it*" [italics added].[3] Franklin no doubt understood what a daunting challenge keeping a republic that was founded on the grand notions of equality and freedom would be to future generations, and he left that challenge for future generations to contemplate. Although several generations removed from Franklin, Abraham Lincoln, too, understood the challenge of holding together the Republic. For Lincoln the challenge was not theoretical, but very real. In his Gettysburg Address, Lincoln described America's civil war as a contest to see whether America "or any nation so conceived and so dedicated, can long endure."[4]

But somewhere along the line we have lost this sense that our democracy is in the trembling hands of humanity rather than the sure hands of fate. The result is that too many young people have come to view the story of America and, indeed, the world, as a litany of heroic exploits by men (and, on the rare occasion, women) to whom they cannot relate and with whom they have nothing in common. History bores them because it is not about them. They need not worry about things such as civil and human rights, freedoms, civic responsibility, stewardship of the environment, care of ancient and modern artifacts, or public and community service because someone else—someone pre-ordained by Destiny—will step forward to take care of those things. The way we teach history, after all, would seem to prove that this has always been the case.

What we need is a new generation of history teachers who will fight for a curriculum that demands that students think and grapple with the crises and challenges of the past. Such a curriculum will never be imposed from the top-down, because it is almost always against the rational self interest of those with power that such a curriculum exist. There is a reason, after all, that the slave owners of the American south were so fearful of educating their slaves. The story of Moses, as we know from Negro spirituals and the testimony of former slaves is hardly a call for submitting to "master." The story of America, like the story of Gandhi, Christ, Jefferson, King, Crazy Horse, and countless others written across the pages of history, is hardly the story of submission. It is the story of men and women struggling for equality and dignity and demanding their fair share. The author H.G. Wells said that civilization was the race between education and catastrophe. In social studies classrooms across this nation, we are losing this race.

The kind of teachers we need is exemplified by a former student of mine named John Daniel. John is passionate, articulate and possesses an awe-inspiring grasp of historical content knowledge, particularly about World War Two. John was a friend and student of the late Stephen Ambrose at the University of New Orleans (UNO), and as a result he knows full-well the power of challenging and thought-provoking history. He is also unwavering and uncompromising in his standards and expectations.

John teaches in a difficult environment, to say the least. He began teaching history in 1998 in the Young Marine program in New Orleans. Here John worked to inspire, motivate and educate young lives that had already been labeled unredeemable and cast aside by many in society. Unhappy with the curriculum he was handed (which included such inane fare as memorizing the rank and pay structures of the US Marine Corps), John ventured out on his own, so to speak, in what he taught his students. Although most of his students were of middle school age, 42 out of the 50 could not read at a third grade level. Rather than continue to sell these young people short, John bravely gave them a two-hour lecture on the history of the US military in the 20th century. His lecture was filled with John's passion and knowledge for the subject and his unique gift for storytelling. Infusing his class with romance, John hoped to garner even a small amount of interest from these kids. For those of you who just became apoplectic in the name of constructivism that John dared *lecture* (a foul epithet in most teacher preparation programs), John understood—as did Whitehead—that you can't ask students to think if they have nothing about which *to* think. The next class, John got his first question from a student. This, as he puts it, "indicated some interest."

I taught John at UNO, and one of the stories he told about capturing the interest of his students has stuck with me to this day. He "teased" these middle school kids as they began studying World War Two by telling them that telephone poles had started that terrible war. Needless to say such a strange assertion caught these students by surprise and piqued their interest; they wanted to know whether their teacher knew what he was talking about or if he was simply crazy. As part of the reparations imposed by the Treaty of Versailles, Germany was required to deliver telephone poles to replace the ones destroyed or damaged in World War One. This was the first condition of that treaty on which the German government reneged. Soon the Germans would be ignoring prohibitions on rebuilding their military, and soon the world would be engulfed in the flames of World War Two. John may be accused of being slightly melodramatic in asserting that the phone poles led to the war, but it worked. He grabbed his students' attention with creativity and imagination and then he did something truly remarkable—he taught them. Before long, John had students comparing Hitler to Genghis Kahn. When John asked the student how he knew about Kahn, the boy replied, "I watch the History Channel, too, you know." As John told me, "I almost cried at that point."

When pressured to focus on literacy with his students, John eschewed the usual phonics exercises and instead had his students practice by learning to read the Declaration of Independence. As he told me, getting them to see that this document was more than an abstraction and that it mattered in their lives was a key point of the activity. Once a student had mastered the document, John went with them online to the National Archives website, where they were able to "sign" the Declaration themselves. He printed it out and sent it away with them. No doubt his colleagues thought him naïve and foolish. What was the chance that these cast-offs who were barely reading at a third grade level (if that) would be able to master the language and the subtle arguments of Jefferson? No doubt he was told that he was wasting his time—best to focus on the basics and be done with it. But John refused to give up on his students and he refused to give up on the transformative power of *good history*. The result is that John Daniel made a difference.

What John understood is what all good history teachers understand—that history is power. Those who control the narrative of a nation control the nation. With this in mind, it is well past time that we reform the dreadful state of history in our nation's schools and take back America's story. Our first step is a simple and obvious one: let's dispense with the so-called *social studies* curriculum and teach history. As I have said earlier, this is in no way a call for the abandonment of the other social sciences such as political science, anthropology, psychology, or geography. Rather, this opinion is based on the common sense principal that it is better to do one thing well than many things poorly. I maintain that one cannot teach history well without these powerful tools being employed. The current effort to dabble in all the social sciences over the course of a 13 year curriculum, however, has produced nothing but confusion.

The second step, again, is to teach history from a constructivist philosophical foundation. Delving into and wrestling with the complexities and often-frustrating contradictions of history is a great preparation for active participation in a democratic society. The way history is currently taught doesn't do this, however, even though that is its expressed aim. As it is taught now, history is jingoistic and slightly Orwellian. It is time to bury the remnants of the Hampton Method once and for all. Thomas Jesse Jones was correct in sensing that open-ended historical inquiry could lead to dangerous things, but he was wrong to believe that such things threatened America. Indeed, just as Martin Luther King, Jr. quoted America's Founders and founding documents in order to shame a nation away from the disgrace of Jim Crow, knowledge of history is the one guarantee that this nation will never settle for less than the highest of our ideals and expectations. John Daniel wanted to take Jefferson's words and make them meaningful to his students. We must all reach for the same lofty goal.

By a constructivist foundation, I do not mean the touchy-feely garbage that has crept into the classroom under such a guise. The teacher has a definite place to play and role in the construction of knowledge. Although constructivism asks us as educators to surrender the final outcome of our work, it manifestly *does not* ask us to simply be passive on-lookers in our classroom. As we have seen with the model provided by Alfred North Whitehead, the role of the teacher, especially in constructivism, is crucial to the future success of our students.

Finally, the history we teach must be the history of all our people. This is not, as some would argue, a recipe for a curriculum of guilt and shame, but a chance to broaden our students' understandings of the contributions of all the groups who have made up and continue to make up this nation. As Christine Bennett has written, "...educational excellence in our schools cannot be achieved without equity."[5] The "Balkanization" of America that many of the anti-diversity folks decry is not the result of including stories of American Indians, African Americans, Hispanic Americans or other groups in our educational discourse. Rather, it is precisely the opposite. The fact that so many groups feel left out of the historical narrative is a major impetus to feelings of disassociation and aloofness towards the nation. Understanding the complex diversity of America will lead to more unity, not less.

The study of history will never be without controversy, nor should it be. The fight over who we were is essentially a fight over who we are. I titled this book *Now More than Ever* which, while slightly hyperbolic, is also partly true. Once again we find ourselves as Americans debating what it means to be American. That troubling old question between freedom and security is again at the heart of our national discourse. The communists fell and we celebrated, but it was less than a decade before the shadowy new enemy of religious fundamentalism reared its head and demanded attention. Combating terrorism has clearly placed before Americans the difficulty of remaining a free society. We are now being asked to decide if we desire to protect America at the cost of sacrificing what it means *to be* American.

It is remarkable that against such a backdrop the systematic study of history—*all history*—is being trimmed from our nation's school systems. Math and science remain the favored curricular foci. As studies continue to mount showing that we are becoming a nation of obese children and adults, those arguing for the return of strict physical education in our schools have ample evidence to throw before school boards. Corporations are loudly complaining that they are forced to hire young graduates who do not know how to write properly, and so literacy and writing get attention. But history seems to have little voice. Perhaps it is because the fundamental questions being asked about whom we are and what our values should be are intended to be rhetorical by the politicians and demagogues who ask them. Whatever the reason, we have entered a new century with new challenges, threats, and promises. History will not provide us with definitive answers, but it may provide us with the necessary courage to begin asking the proper questions without fear of where such inquiry might take us.

Shortly before her death in 1917, Liliuokalani, the last monarch of the Kingdom of Hawaii, gave an important and powerful job to her foster daughter. "She extracted a promise from Lydia," writes Liliuokalani's biographer Helena G. Allen, "to tell her 'true and complete story.' 'My story is a universal one,' she said. 'The same betrayal of all peoples can happen if 'they' do not understand.'"[6] Tell the story, she begged, that others may learn. This is the cry of history, and this is the cause of history. To come forward and pronounce to the world that you are or wish to become a history teacher is a noble and, one would hope, humbling thing. It is to announce that you wish to be the keeper of the stories, and that you can be trusted with the tales of the men who stormed Normandy and the generations of others who have succeeded, failed, and tried for greatness.

The men and women who have come before us deserve better than the treatment they currently receive. Their story is ours. Let us dedicate ourselves to telling it in a way that is passionate, accurate and full. We are part of a continuum that stretches from Herodotus and Plutarch to Schlesinger and Ellis. It has been a grand tradition, we need only to remember. The necessary reform of history will not come quickly and it will not come easily. Battered by ideologues from the Left and the Right, teachers of history will need strong wills and thick skin. But reform we must and the process should begin immediately. Robert Kennedy was fond of telling a story to his audiences that illustrated the need for action. He said:

> The great French marshal [Louis-Hubert-Gonzalve] Lyautey once asked his gardener to plant a tree. The gardener objected that the tree was slow growing and would not reach maturity for one hundred years. The marshal replied, "In that case, there's no time to lose. Plant it this afternoon."[7]

Our garden needs work, and there is no time like the present to rescue our past.

---

1 Maxwell Taylor Kennedy, Ed. *Make Gentle the Life of this World: The Vision of Robert F. Kennedy* (New York: Harcourt Brace and Company, 1998), 3.
2 Joseph J. Ellis, *Founding Brothers: The Revolutionary Generation* (New York: Vintage Books, 2000), 78.
3 Walter Isaacson, *Benjamin Franklin: An American Life* (New York: Simon and Schuster, 2003), 459.
4 Maureen Harrison and Steve Gilbert (Eds.), *Abraham Lincoln: In His Own Words* (New York: Barnes and Noble Books, 1994), 347.
5 Christine I. Bennett, *Comprehensive Multicultural Education: Theory and Practice Fifth Edition* (Boston: Allyn and Bacon, 2003), 18.
6 Helena G. Allen, *The Betrayal of Liliuokalani, Last Queen of Hawaii 1838-1917* (Honolulu, HI: Mutual Publishing, 1982), 17.
7 Kennedy, *Make Gentle the Life of This World*, 6.

Select Bibliography

Allen, Helena G. *The Betrayal of Liluokalani, Last Queen of Hawaii, 1838-1917.* Honolulu, HI: Mutual Publishing, 1982.
Alterman, Eric. *What Liberal Media? The Truth About Bias and the News.* New York: Basic Books, 2003.
Armstrong, David G., and Tom V. Savage. *Teaching in the Secondary School, An Introduction.* Upper Saddle River, NJ: Merrill, 1998.
Axtell, James. *The Indian Peoples of Eastern America: A Documentary History of the Sexes.* Oxford: Oxford University Press, 1981.
Barr, Robert, James L. Barth, and S. Samuel Shermis. *Defining the Social Studies.* Bulletin 51. Washington, D.C.: National Council for the Social Studies, 1977.
Bennett, Christine I. *Comprehensive Multicultural Education: Theory and Practice.* Boston: Allyn and Bacon, 2003.
Boehm, Richard G. *States and Regions.* New York: Harcourt Brace and Company, 2000.
Bruce, Tammy. *The New Thought Police: Inside the Left's Assault on Free Speech and Free Minds.* New York: Random House, 2001.
Bryant, Jr., James A. *A Noble Discontent: The Experiences and Perceptions of Seven Pre-Service Teachers in an Experimental Course Designed to Examine the Relationship Between Social Consciousness and Education.* Unpublished doctoral dissertation, The University of North Dakota, 2003.
Campbell, Will D. *Brother to a Dragonfly.* New York: Contiuum, 2000.
Clowse, Barbara Barksdale. *Brainpower for the Cold War: The Sputnik Crisis and National Defense Act of 1958.* Westport, Conn.: Greenwood Press, 1981.
Cowley, Robert, ed. *What Ifs? of American History: Eminent Historians Imagine What Might Have Been.* New York: G.P. Putnam's Sons, 2003.
Day, Dorothy. *The Long Loneliness.* New York: Harper and Row, 1952.
Dean, John W. *Worse Than Watergate: The Secret Presidency of George W. Bush.* New York: Little, Brown and Company, 2004.
Dewey, John. *Experience and Education.* New York: Touchstone Books, 1997.
Dewey, John. *Democracy and Education: An Introduction to the Philosophy of Education.* New York: The Free Press, 1916.
DuBois, W.E.B. *The Education of Black People: Ten Critiques, 1906-1960.* New York: Monthly Review Press, 1973.

Dynneson, Thomas L., and Richard E. Gross. *Designing Effective Instruction for Secondary Social Studies*. Upper Saddle River, NJ: Merrill, 1999.

Ellis, Joseph J. *Founding Brothers: The Revolutionary Generation*. New York: Vintage Books, 2000.

Emerson, Ralph Waldo. *Selected Writings of Ralph Waldo Emerson*. New York: New American Library, 1965.

Engelhardt, Tom, and Edward T. Linenthal, eds. *History Wars: The Enola Gay and other Battles for the American Past*. New York: Henry Holt and Company, 1996.

Farmer, David Hugh. *The Oxford Dictionary of Saints, Third Edition*. Oxford: Oxford University Press, 1992.

Gandhi, Mohondas K. *An Autobiography: The Story of my Experiments with Truth*. Mahadev Desai, Translator. Boston: Beacon Press, 1993.

Gathercoal, Forrest. *Judicious Discipline*. San Francisco: Caddo Gap Press, 2004.

Giroux, Henry A. *Ideology, Culture, and the Process of Schooling*. (Philadelphia: Temple University Press, 1981.

Hamilton, Edith. *The Greek Way*. New York: W.W. Norton, 1993.

Hansen, David T. *The Call to Teach*. New York: Teachers College Press, 1995.

Harrison, Maureen, and Steve Gilbert, eds. *Abraham Lincoln: In His Own Words*. New York: Barnes and Noble Books, 1994.

Hart, Gary. *Restoration of the Republic: The Jeffersonian Ideal in 21st Century America*. Oxford: Oxford University Press, 2002.

Hart, Gary. *The Patriot: An Exhortation to Liberate America from the Barbarians*. New York: The Free Press, 1996.

Henke, Robin R., Susan P. Choy, Xianglei Chen, Sonya Geis, Martha Naomi Alt, and Stephen P. Broughman. *America's Teachers: Profile of a Profession, 1993-94*. Washington, D.C.: U.S. Department of Education, 1997.

Howard, Gary R. *We Can't Teach What We Don't Know: White Teachers, Multiracial Schools*. New York: Teachers College Press, 1999.

Hurston, Zora Neale. *Dust Tracks on a Road: An Autobiography*. New York: HarperPerrenial, 1991.

Issacson, Walter. *Benjamin Franklin: An American Life*. New York: Simon and Schuster, 2003.

Jackson, Kenneth T. *Building a History Curriculum: Guidelines for Teaching History in Schools*. Westlake, OH: National Council for History Education Inc., 2003.

Kennedy, Maxwell Taylor, ed. *Make Gentle the Life of this World: The Vision of Robert F. Kennedy*. New York: Harcourt Brace and Company, 1998.

Klee, Mary Beth. "Are They Too Young for History?" *History Matters!* 17 No.4 (December 2004), 1.

Kohl, Herbert. *On Teaching*. New York: Schocken Books, 1976.

Lame Deer, Archie Fire, and Richard Erdoes. *Gift of Power: The Life and Teachings of a Lakota Medicine Man*. Sante Fe: Bear and Company, 1992.

Laughlin, Margaret A., and H. Michael Hartoonian. *Challenges of Social Studies Instruction in Middle and High Schools*. New York: Harcourt Brace College Publishers, 1995.

Lindsey, Donal F. *Indians at Hampton Institute 1877-1923*. Chicago: University of Illinois Press, 1995.

Loeb, Paul Rogat. *Soul of a Citizen: Living with Conviction in a Cynical Time*. New York: St. Martin's Griffin, 1999.

Loewen, James W. *Lies My Teacher Told Me: Everything Your American History Textbook Got Wrong.* New York: Touchstone Books, 1995.

Martin, Jay. *The Education of John Dewey: A Biography.* New York: Columbia University Press, 2002.

Marx, Karl, and Friedrich Engels. *The Communist Manifesto.* New York: Signet Classic, 1998.

Maxim, George W. *Dynamic Social Studies for Constructivist Classrooms: Inspiring Tomorrow's Social Scientists.* Upper Saddle River, NJ: Merrill, 2006.

McDonnell, Thomas P., ed. *A Thomas Merton Reader.* New York: Image Books, 1989.

McDougall, Walter A. "The Three Reasons We Must Teach History." *History Matters!* 17 No.2 (October 2004), 7.

McNeil, John D. *Curriculum: The Teacher's Initiative.* Upper Saddle River, NJ: Merrill, 1999.

Nash, Gary B., Charlotte Crabtree and Ross E. Dunn. *History on Trial: Culture Wars and the Teaching of the Past.* New York: Vintage Books, 2000.

Niebuhr, Reinhold. *Moral Man and Immoral Society: A Study in Ethics and Politics.* Louisville, KY: Westminster John Knox Press, 2001.

Noll, James William, ed. *Taking Sides: Clashing Views on Controversial Educational Issues.* Guilford, CT: Dushkin/McGraw Hill, 2001.

Palmer, Parker J. *The Courage to Teach: Exploring the Inner Landscape of a Teacher's Life.* San Francisco: Jossey-Bass, 1991.

Perrone, Vito. *Lessons for New Teachers.* Boston: McGraw-Hill, 2000.

Perrone, Vito. *A Letter to Teachers: Reflections on schooling and the art of teaching.* San Francisco: Jossey-Bass, 1991.

Postman, Neil, and Charles Weingartner. *Teaching as a Subversive Activity: A no-holds barred assault on outdated teaching methods—with dramatic and practical proposals on how education can be made relevant to today's world.* New York: Delacorte Press, 1969.

Powell, William S. *North Carolina: A Proud State in our Nation.* Evanston, IL: McDougal Littell, 2003.

Pullias, Earl V., and J.D. Young. *A Teacher is Many Things.* Bloomington, IN: Indiana University Press, 1968.

Raphael, Ray. *The Teacher's Voice: A Sense of Who We Are.* (Portsmouth, NH: Heinemann, 1985.

Ravitch, Diane. *The Language Police: How Pressure Groups Restrict What Students Learn.* New York: Alfred A. Knopf, 2003.

Ravitch, Diane. "Who Prepares our History Teachers? Who Should Prepare our History Teachers?" Keynote Address, National Council for History Education. October 18, 1997.

Russell, Ronny. *Can a Church Live Again? The Revitalization of a 21st Century Church.* Macon, GA: Smyth and Helwys, 2004.

Schlesinger, Jr., Arthur M. *Robert Kennedy and his Times.* New York: Ballantine Books, 1978.

Spring, Joel. *American Education.* Boston: McGraw-Hill Higher Education, 2000.

Stanislavski, Constantine. *Creating a Role.* New York: Routledge Press, 2003.

Tanner, Daniel, and Laurel Tanner. *Curriculum Development: Theory into Practice.* Upper Saddle River, NJ: Merrill, 1995.

Toobin, Jeffrey. *A Vast Conspiracy: The Real Story of the Sex Scandal That Nearly Brought Down a President.* New York: Random House, 1999.

Vella, Jane. *Learning to Listen, Learning to Teach: The Power of Dialogue in Educating Adults.* San Francisco: Jossey-Bass, 1994.

Vygotsky, L.S. *Mind in Society: The Development of Higher Psychological Processes.* Cambridge, Mass.: Harvard University Press, 1978.

Wells, Melinda. *Teacher educators' conceptions of the responsibility of teachers as moral educators.* Unpublished doctoral dissertation, Boston University, 1998.

Whitehead, Alfred North. *The Aims of Education and Other Essays.* New York: The Free Press, 1929.

About the Author

James A. Bryant, Jr. is an Assistant Professor for Curriculum and Instruction at Appalachian State University. He holds a Ph.D. in Education from the University of North Dakota. He lives in western North Carolina with his wife, Ginger, and their children Cheyenne, Autumn, and James.

Also by the Author

Curley

Curley is a novel based on the life of Russell Norris, a Cherokee Indian from the Qualla Boundary reservation in western North Carolina. After Russell and his family move from the reservation to Cramerton, North Carolina, a textile mill town, Russell's father takes a job as a foreman in the Cramer Cotton Mill. When Russell is only fifteen-years-old, his father dies, leaving the responsibility of raising and supporting the family on Russell's young shoulders. Determined not to die in the same mill as his father, Russell packs his guitar and hits the road, supporting his mother and four brothers by playing music throughout the southeastern United States. Traveling and working in the Depression-era South, Russell is forced to confront racism and his own battle and alcoholism. Ultimately, this is a story of courage, hope and redemption.

ISBN 0-7618-2806-0
www.univpress.com/hamiltonbooks

www.ingramcontent.com/pod-product-compliance
Lightning Source LLC
Chambersburg PA
CBHW021132300426
44113CB00006B/398